CARNAL Christians

and other words that don't go together

RICH WILKERSON

CARNAL CHRISTIANS
And Other Words That Don't Go Together

Rich Wilkerson
P.O. Box 1092
Tacoma, Washington 98401

Copyright © 1986 by Rich Wilkerson
Printed in the United States of America
ISBN: 0-88368-188-9

*Writing and editorial assistance
by Donna C. Arthur*

DEDICATION

This book is dedicated to my father, The Reverend John Wilkerson, and my father-in-law, The Reverend Fulton Buntain. They taught me to love God, the Church, and the lost.

In Appreciation:

To my wife Robyn for her God-given ability to administrate our home, office staff, and crusade ministry while I am so often on the road.

To Donna Arthur for her great help in assimilating my messages and thoughts into written form.

And to Bob Whitaker for publishing this book on holiness. May God bless you all!

CONTENTS

INTRODUCTION

Recently I saw a sign that said, "Wanted—clean fill dirt." I thought, Those words don't go together. How can you get clean dirt?

Since pastoring, counseling, and traveling in a fulltime evangelistic ministry, I have talked with people whose ideas are like that sign. Their lives are full of impure mixtures. Sometimes they are referred to as "carnal Christians."

A carnal person's life is governed by bodily pleasures and appetites. But a person who commits his life to Jesus Christ should be able to say, "I am crucified with Christ: nevertheless I live; yet not I, but Christ liveth in me: and the life which I now live in the flesh I live by the faith of the Son of God, who loved me, and gave himself for me" (Galatians 2:20).

To suggest that a person can be both Christian and carnal is not only incorrect but impossible.

The following situations have actually happened.

* A young woman told me that God led her to sleep with her boyfriend to deepen their love relationship. She said, "Of course, we have prayer and Bible study first."

* A man responded to my question, "Are

9

you a Christian?'' with this answer—
''Well, sort of.'' I replied, ''SORT OF?
Did Christ 'sort of' die for you?''

* A girl came to the altar one night boldly
proclaiming her love for God. ''Yes, I
love God, but I hate my parents,'' she
later said.

An impure mixture of thoughts has invaded the
church. We mix things that cannot be mixed. Oddly
enough, Scripture tells us this discord is the prelude
to the last days. Daniel 2:41-43 speaks of the impure
mixture of ''iron mixed with miry clay.'' The passage
refers to a kingdom that is partly strong and partly
broken.

Daniel 2:44 says, ''And in the days of these kings shall
the God of heaven set up a kingdom, which shall never
be destroyed: and the kingdom shall not be left to other
people, but it shall break in pieces and consume all
these kingdoms, and it shall stand for ever.'' Hallelujah! That is what we as Christians are believing God
for—a pure and strong kingdom.

The purpose of this book is to help those who have
entertained the idea that it is possible to follow Christ
but continue to live a carnal lifestyle. I pray that, as you
read, God will help you to uproot and destroy this idea.

''Therefore if any man be in Christ, he is a new
creature: old things are passed away; behold, all things
are become new'' (2 Corinthians 5:17).

Can a person be both carnal and Christlike?

''For to be carnally minded is death; but to be
spiritually minded is life and peace. Because the car-

nal mind is enmity against God; for it is not subject to the law of God, neither indeed can be" (Romans 8:6-7).

I believe it is impossible to follow both Christ and your own sensual desires. God has told us that "through the Spirit" we might "mortify the deeds of the body" (Romans 8:13).

It *is* possible to live your life in a way pleasing to God, and the following pages will tell you how.

PART I

The Problem

Chapter 1

INNOCENT IDOLATRY

Innocent idolatry, what a combination. If there were ever two words that don't go together, they would have to be "innocent idolatry." The enemy of our souls, however, has reverted to such subtle tactics today that he has taken the good things of life and turned them against the Christian community. Many Christians have fallen prey to these "innocent idols."

What do you think of when you hear the word *idol?*

Do you imagine a squatting, sad-faced wooden statue?

Have you seen any of these pagan patrons carried into church lately or sitting on someone's desk at work? No, you probably haven't. But if you did, I'm sure you could easily identify one of these cult-like images.

One of the problems within the church today is that Christians are worshipping false idols; but these idols are so subtle, we fail to recognize them.

How does idol worship begin in the church? Do you think Christians are one day walking close to

15

the Lord and the next day following after error?

I believe we enter into idolatry the same way Israel did—by continual peer pressure. Living in the midst of a heathen nation, Israel listened to the voices of the mixed multitude and succumbed to their pressure.

Christians are also living in the midst of an ungodly civilization, and the pressure to conform is overwhelming. Do you know I have never received a letter from someone saying, "Rich, help me. I'm being pressured into having a Bible study." Instead, continual, negative peer pressure causes many people to serve the god of this world. Peer pressure is simply a man-made, modern term for that old word—temptation.

God spoke clearly to Israel. He said, "Thou shalt have no other gods before me" (Exodus 20:3). God's first commandment to Moses is still the first commandment today. God calls us to obedience. He does not ask us to logically decipher every detail. "Behold, to obey is better than sacrifice" (1 Samuel 15:22).

Identifying Idols

How then can we begin to recognize our own areas of idolatry?

First, we need to understand the word *idol*. An idol is an object of extreme devotion. It does not have to be an object carved out of stone. Idols can be made up of the good things in our life—things that we have placed before our relationship to the living God.

Unfortunately, one of man's chief idols can be his own service to God. Paul said in Galatians 3:3, "Are ye so foolish? having begun in the Spirit, are ye now made perfect by the flesh?" Sometimes a person starts out full of power for God, but soon the method of that ministry becomes the focal point of service and worship rather than God.

Prior to the cross, the apostle Peter worshipped his ministry before he worshipped Christ. Peter enjoyed the good life! Let's picture it.

Jesus said in Matthew 10:11, "And into whatsoever city or town ye shall enter, inquire who in it is worthy; and there abide till ye go thence."

In verse 8 of that same chapter, Jesus also told them, "Heal the sick, cleanse the lepers, raise the dead, cast out devils: freely ye have received, freely give."

Think what it would mean if you were to go into a city as a man or woman of God and, because of your ministry, eliminate all of that city's problems. No more drug addiction or alcoholism would exist. The hospitals and the morgues would be emptied. I mean we are talking about a city that has been put back together again!

Don't you think the mayor would want to take you to dinner and give you the keys to the city? Don't you think people would invite you to their homes for a free dinner? Don't you think you would be invited to stay in the finest homes available and have 24-hour maid service?

What I am trying to say is that, prior to the cross, Jesus and the disciples had anywhere from 5,000 to 20,000 people at their meetings. They had it made!

As chief of staff, Peter was their henchman, the hard guy, the one who yelled to "get those kids out of here." Peter had it made! But Peter began to worship his lifestyle. He worshipped what he had, what he did, and the kind of charisma and clout he had from being with the Lord.

Somewhere Peter missed Christ and caught on to his idol—his ministry in the work of Christ. So much so that Peter boastfully said, "I'll never forsake you Lord; though all men forsake you, I'll never forsake you. You can count on me." How do we know all this must be true? Well, later on at the time of the crucifixion, Peter cursed the name of Jesus and denied the Lord three times.

That's not something you do to someone you've worshipped. Peter had ended up making an idol out of a good thing—the ministry—the work of God, the call of God.

While my father was in seminary, he had a close friend who was an extraordinary communicator. After traveling and pastoring for several years, this man ended up on the West Coast with a successful counseling ministry. Unfortunately, he, like Peter, began to worship his ministry. It wasn't long before he lost his wife, his children, and his ministry because of his misdirected devotion. He is still in the professional counseling field today, but he is far from God. This man started out loving God, but a lot of good "things" became his object of worship.

Here is my point: graven images are obvious idols. Christians can recognize those and run from error. Our problems begin because we *cannot* recognize that we are idolizing the good things God has given us instead of worshipping the Giver.

Are You My God?

Another innocent idol of this age is the *love of money*. Richard Foster says in his book *Money, Sex, and Power:* "Compulsive extravagance is a modern mania. The contemporary lust for 'more, more, more' is clearly psychotic; it has completely lost touch with reality. The chasm between Third World poverty and First World affluence is accelerating at an alarming rate. And many earnest believers are at a loss to know what to do in the midst of these perplexing realities."[1]

Jesus said in Luke 6:24, "Woe unto you that are rich." In Matthew 6:19, He said, "Lay not up for yourselves treasures upon earth." In Matthew 19:24, Jesus said, "It is easier for a camel to go through the eye of a needle, than for a rich man to enter into the kingdom of God."

I have heard people say, "Yes, but God has led me to make a lot of money so I can help the work of God." If you compare what most of those people are earning with what they're giving, it's a joke. God is not impressed with a person who is only looking for a tax write-off.

When money, rather than God, becomes a person's reason for living, he has moved into idolatry. I know one man who has made more money than he can spend in ten lifetimes. In fact, I know ten men who have made more than they can spend in ten lifetimes. Yet for some, their only goal is to get another million.

On the last day of their lives, Howard Hughes and Aristotle Onassis were still figuring out how to make more money. Incredible!

David said to Araunah, "Neither will I offer burnt offerings unto the Lord my God of that which doth cost me nothing" (2 Samuel 24:24). In other words, David was saying, my gifts to God are going to cost me something. After all my wonderful Lord has done for me, I want to give Him something that will represent my hard work and effort. My object of worship is the living God and not the fruits of my labor.

Christ said to the church at Laodicea, "I know thy works, that thou art neither cold nor hot: I would thou wert cold or hot. So then because thou art lukewarm, and neither cold nor hot, I will spue thee out of my mouth. Because thou sayest, I am rich, and increased with goods, and have need of nothing ... " (Revelation 3:15-17).

Blinded by extravagance, the church at Laodicea could not see their need. But Jesus continued, "And knowest not that thou art wretched, and miserable, and poor, and blind, and naked" (Revelation 3:17).

Money is a tool. It sustains us physically and can be used to reach souls for Christ. *But money must not be an object of worship.*

How Important Am I?

Another god of this generation is the *god of status*. Innocent idolators say, "When I achieve a higher position, then I'll share Jesus with others. I'll be respected and, therefore, others will listen to my message." It doesn't work that way.

I've spoken to nearly a million students nationwide in public school assemblies. God has opened some difficult doors. Often the hardest schools for me to get into are those with "born-again" principals!

Many of these principals were convinced they would be warriors for God once they rose to their high positions. But when I contact them, tell them what I intend to present and that I am a Christian, they won't let me in their schools. Even when I explain that my presentation is not religious and conforms to public education's regulations, they are still intimidated by their own system.

Do what you are going to do for God now—because in ten years, even with more status, you won't be any different. If you're not going to witness for Christ while you're a freshman in college, you're not going to witness for Him when you finally become an attorney, doctor, or teacher.

Some say, "I'm going to study for the ministry and become a missionary to Africa. That's when I'll really start sharing Christ." Let me tell you something—Africa begins one step out of your front door. If you don't witness for Christ here, you're not going to do it over there.

This god of status has invaded Christian leadership as well. I'm thinking of one city with two separate churches. Both pastors are very successful, but their emphasis is so different. Recently I sat on the stage with one of these pastors. He said, "Do you see that man sitting over there? He's a doctor. And that woman sitting over there is a lawyer. And that person in the second row gave over $100,000 to the church. And that man just walking in the door is the head of the local school board." This pastor placed an incredible emphasis on status.

In the other church in that city, people jam the church to the rafters singing, praising, and loving God. It's a blue-collar-type church. They are paying cash for their building by taking offerings.

When I visited this pastor's church, his emphasis was entirely different. He said, "See that lady? She was once a prostitute, but Christ changed her life. Incredible story! See that man that just walked in? He was divorced and an alcoholic. But God saved him, delivered him from alcohol, and restored his marriage. Incredible miracle! See that woman in the front seat? She has six kids to support—their father was recently imprisoned for molesting his children. That woman now gets up at 4:30 every morning, gets those kids out of bed, gets them all dressed and fed, takes them to school, and then goes to work. After work she picks them all up, takes them home, fixes their supper, and puts them to bed. They are living on a shoestring, but she is trusting God."

One pastor was impressed by status, and the other was impressed by changed lives.

Status can become a god.

> My brethren ... if there come unto your assembly a man with a gold ring, in goodly apparel, and there come in also a poor man in vile raiment; and ye have respect to him that weareth the gay clothing, and say unto him, Sit thou here in a good place; and say to the poor, Stand thou there, or sit here under my footstool: are you not then partial in yourselves, and are become judges of evil thoughts?
>
> Hearken, my beloved brethren, Hath not God chosen the poor of this world rich in faith, and heirs of the kingdom which he hath promised to them that love him? But ye have despised the poor. Do not rich men oppress you, and draw you before the judgment seats? Do not they blaspheme that worthy name by the which ye are called?
>
> If ye fulfil the royal law according to the scripture, Thou shalt love thy neighbor as thyself, ye do well: But if ye have respect to persons, ye commit sin, and are convinced of the law as transgressors (James 2:1-9).

I am a member of a great church in Tacoma, Washington. It's a beautiful mix of wealthy and

23

poor, lower and middle class. Several years ago, a woman, who had only accepted Christ weeks before, was asked to sing during our Sunday morning service. She came from the nightclub world, had been far from God, and had some very sad things take place in her life.

She was a beautiful, new creation in Jesus Christ. But as she stood to sing before several thousand people, I watched some eyebrows raise. Not knowing any different, she had dressed for the nightclub crowd even though it was Sunday morning. Then she began to sing "No One Ever Cared For Me Like Jesus." By the time she finished, rich and poor, high and low, middle class and lower class all wept together. In that moment a beautiful illustration was made real to our congregation—status means little in light of the grace of God.

Status must not be our idol because Jesus is our Lord.

Oh, Thou God Of Higher Knowledge ...

I am the vice-president of Northwest College in Seattle, Washington—a small, private Christian school with about seven hundred students. One of our battles is knowing how to become knowledgeable and still remain sweet, humble, and loving before our Savior.

The devil would like to substitute education and knowledge in place of the moving of God's Spirit. Science believes if something cannot be defined, it isn't real. However, listen to the words of A. W. Tozer: "The witness of the church is most effective when she declares rather than explains, for the gospel is addressed not to reason but to faith. What can be proved requires no faith to accept. Faith rests upon the character of God, not upon the demonstration of laboratory or logic."[2]

Therefore, a Christian must write in his heart what is written in God's Word. Thus saith the Lord, "This is the way, walk ye in it ... " (Isaiah 30:21). The very thing that makes a college or a church great may be the thing that causes its demise—the simple question, why?

What has caused us to question things that should not be questioned?

The Bible says, "Knowledge puffeth up" (1 Corinthians 8:1). I thank God for educated teachers and learned men and women. But our learning should never cause us to be cynical, puffed up, proud, or arrogant.

Paul said, "I count my life as dung that I might win Christ." Paul was a learned man. In 2 Corinthians 11 you find a brief history of Paul's lineage and background as a Jew. Trained not only in higher education but also through countless experiences, Paul expressed gratitude just to be a man of God.

Please don't misunderstand my intentions here. More than ever, the church is in need of leaders who have perservered in higher education. The apostle said, "Study to show thyself approved unto God, a workman that needeth not to be ashamed, rightly dividing the word of truth" (2 Timothy 2:15). But that quest for knowledge must be subject to the sweet promptings of the Holy Spirit in our lives.

Pursuing The "Good Life"

The Bible tells us that in the last days *pleasure and leisure will become the god of many*. "This know also, that in the last days perilous times shall come. For men shall be ... lovers of pleasures more than lovers of God" (2 Timothy 3:1-4). Paul wrote to Titus saying, "For we ourselves also were sometimes foolish, disobedient, deceived, serving divers lusts and pleasures" (Titus 3:3). Hebrews 11:25 talks about "enjoying the pleasures of sin for a season."

Do you know what bothers me? Christians are also yielding to the god of pleasure and leisure. Yes, they attend church on Sunday morning. Yes, they sound and look the part. But many Christians are so given to living the good life and having it all that they don't bear any fruit for God.

I hear it said, "We need to be together more with our family. We need to have more good times with the family. That's why we aren't going to be in church on Sunday (or at that retreat or at that weekly meeting)."

I knew a man who was a devoted Christian. One day he decided that he was working too many hours and needed to spend more time with his family. Every Friday after work, he, his wife, and his kids would load up their motor home and head for the mountains for the weekend. Before long, "family time" replaced the Sunday morning worship hour. It became the object of his worship.

He excused himself by saying, "God called me to be the priest of my family." Let me tell you, it's hard to be the family's priest when you take them to the ski slopes but never spend time in prayer or in teaching God's Word.

Today this man's family is divided, and his kids are far from God. They still get together for Christmas and have a big time, but the Christ of Christmas is not part of their celebration. Spending time together became the object of this family's worship and attention; and, as a result, they lost something of greater value.

Jesus spoke about the negative aspect of pleasure in the parable of the sower. "And that which fell among thorns are they, which, when they have heard, go forth, and are choked with cares and riches and pleasures of this life, and bring no fruit to perfection" (Luke 8:14).

Chasing after the pleasures of this world is like eating cotton candy. Once you touch it, it disappears. Pleasure has no substance. Once a longed-for pleasure has been experienced, it's over. Neither good times nor spent money can be brought back. Instead, additional pleasure must be sought.

God has a better idea. David said in Psalm 16:11, "In thy presence is fulness of joy; at thy right hand there are pleasures for evermore." The need for pleasure is met by living and taking joy in God's presence.

Finding The Treasure

What is God calling His people to do?
God is calling us in this last day to be separate

and holy, to put away these innocent idols once and for all, and to return to the first commandment—''Thou shalt have no other gods before me.''

God is our pursuit. The Bible says David had a heart after God. That word ''after'' in this instance is used as a verb. It meant he was chasing after God. David wanted to be like God.

God's Word tells us Jesus is coming back for a Church without spot or wrinkle. Christians are the Church. ''Wherefore come out from among them, and be ye separate, saith the Lord, and touch not the unclean thing; and I will receive you'' (2 Corinthians 6:17).

A. W. Tozer said in his book, *The Pursuit of God,* ''The man who has God for his treasure has all things in One. Many ordinary treasures may be denied him; or if he is allowed to have them, the enjoyment of them will be so tempered that they will never be necessary to his happiness. Or if he must see them go, one after one, he will scarcely feel a sense of loss, for having the Source of all things, he has in One all satisfaction, all pleasure, all delight. Whatever he may lose he has actually lost nothing for he now has it all in One, and he has it purely, legitimately and forever.''[3]

If we know God, if He is our pursuit, if He is our all in all, then we cannot live the carnal lifestyle of worshipping these so-called innocent idols.

Chapter 2

PRUDENT PARTIERS

Not long ago a man in the church said to me, "Sure I'm gonna serve Christ, but I'm gonna have a good time, too. I live in the age of grace, and I'm not under the law anymore."

Affirming a creed does not make a person a Christian.

I've heard the excuse too often, "Christians aren't perfect, just forgiven." Those who live by this motto believe they can live like the devil all day and ask for forgiveness before they go to sleep at night.

Sin is still sin, regardless of how popular it is. Prudent partiers say it's okay to party if it's done in moderation. How has this thinking crept into the church?

America: Land Of The Cooked Frogs

In the late sixties and early seventies, the use of marijuana was a felony. Later it was changed to a misdemeanor. Although it is still legally a misdemeanor, enforcement of this law is almost unheard of.

America has a multi-billion-dollar drug business. You've no doubt heard the story of the frog who was thrown into a kettle of cold water. The heat was turned up so gradually that he was not aware he was being cooked. The American society is like that frog. We have heard about drugs so often that we've become immune to their widespread use.

Several years ago, I was doing a crusade in northern California. Friends told me that part of the county was known for its homegrown marijuana. The marijuana plants are surrounded by an arsenal of weapons in case of invasion by the police. Marijuana has become the county's leading crop, and the residents simply accept the fact.

A "Pot" Of Deception

A young man said to me several months ago, "Rich, I smoke pot because it helps to expand my mind. It puts me in an atmosphere where I understand God and spend time in peaceful meditation."

Satan desires to suspend people from reality. While a person's mind is suspended, the devil can fill it with fear, deception, lies, and filth. When the person comes down from their drug-induced high, he has a sense of guilt and condemnation rather than peace.

Revelation 21:8 says, "Sorcerers, and idolaters, and all liars, shall have their part in the lake which burneth with fire and brimstone: which is the second death." The word *sorcery* comes from the Greek work "pharmakia" which means both drug use and abuse.

God is not going to let those who insist on destroying themselves with the filth of the enemy inhabit His kingdom.

I have a friend who conducts seminars in high schools. In the mid-seventies, Gary was speaking in a midwestern school. As he walked to the microphone, a young man in the balcony hollered, "Hey, man, did God make marijuana?"

Gary said, "Well, yes, He did."

As soon as he said that, kids all over the auditorium pulled out joints, and a cloud of smoke soon filled the room. The kids were laughing, carrying on, and smoking their dope. Gary didn't know what to do so he just screamed at the top of his lungs, "This is a bust!"

Immediately kids started sitting on their marijuana joints, putting them in their mouths, and swallowing them. Once they had done that, they became quiet.

Gary looked up at the guy who started all this commotion and said, "Hey, man."

The kid said, "What, man?"

Gary said, "Did God make cactus?"

"Well, yeah, He did," the kid replied.

Gary said, "Well, you don't have to sit on it do you?"

At that point the whole place broke into laughter, and Gary had their attention for the remainder of the presentation.

God did make everything on the planet, but we don't have to misuse what God made. And that is what people are doing with marijuana.

I often hear adults say, "Well, kids will be kids.

They'll grow out of this stage."

Let me tell you about a young man who attended the youth group in my church. He came from a wonderful Christian home. He was an obedient son and was involved in activities with the church youth. I was there for five years. When I left, he was seventeen.

This boy's father owned a business in town. One night this young man, now in his early twenties and the manager of his father's business, was closing up when one of his friends drove into the parking lot. Some employees saw the car, but they thought nothing of it and went home.

The next morning when one of the employees came to work, he found this young man lying dead in the lobby. Several days after the funeral, the authorities found the killer. It was one of the young men who had been a pallbearer. He was turned in by his girlfriend. This young man also went to church and had attended a Christian school. These "kids-who-will-be-kids" had been struggling with drugs for a long time.

Some kids never outgrow drug problems. I can take you to some high-rise establishments in New York or Chicago and show you some big kids who are fifty-two years old and have not grown out of it.

A prudent drug user does not exist.

Freedom Or Bondage

Alcohol is America's most deadly drug. Listen to these facts:

* Alcohol causes, directly or indirectly, at least half of the nation's 55,000 traffic deaths each year.
* Approximately 40,000 suicides a year are alcohol related.
* At least half of all arrests in the United States are alcohol related.
* An estimated ten million Americans suffer from alcohol-related diseases and a quarter million of them die each year as a result.
* Alcohol addiction affects an estimated forty million lives—including family, friends, employers, fellow workers—at a yearly cost to the American economy of more than thirty billion dollars.
* An estimated one million five hundred thousand teenagers between the ages of 13 and 17 are alcoholics.

Let's look at what Americans are drinking. Each year they are pouring down their throats:

* 250 million gallons of distilled spirits
* 150 million bottles of beer
* 100 million gallons of wine
* An uncalculated amount of illegal moonshine, whiskey, and homemade beers and wines

I'll never forget sitting with a young minister friend of mine when this topic of drinking came up. He said, "Rich, you drink wine, don't you?"

I said, "No, I don't."

He said, "You're kidding?"

I said, "No."

He looked at me and said, "You know, I was beginning to think I was the last pastor who didn't drink. Everywhere I travel I run into ministers and youth workers who drink and think nothing of it. They say they've been delivered from the bondage of the law. They're free and liberated."

I said, "Well, I know many ministers who have been delivered from the bondage of the law, but those ministers have not placed themselves under the bondage of alcohol either."

Now that I'm traveling nationwide, I see it more and more myself. In this age of liberation, we are free—but are we free simply to come under another heavier bondage?

A recent survey estimated that nearly 71 percent of all American adults drink alcohol in one form or another. That astounds me when you consider that 43 percent of the adult population professes to be born-again Christians. This problem of alcohol has invaded churches in a huge way.

When ministers, youth workers, elders, and deacons drink, is it any wonder that our young people are struggling?

A young man came up to me recently whom I had known for several years. He was a member of a church and attended a Christian school. "Mr. Wilkerson," he said, "please, please help me. I'm an alcoholic." He was fourteen!

I believe that some people can take a drink and

never become an alcoholic. But how do you know which person that might be?

What do you suppose happens to that someone who is susceptible to alcoholism and watches his Christian parents drink socially? One weekend that kid goes out and trys some alcohol with his friends. He enjoys it and does it again, and again, and again. Before long he's hooked.

Jesus said, "But whoso shall offend one of these little ones which believe in me, it were better for him that a millstone were hanged about his neck, and that he were drowned in the depth of the sea" (Matthew 18:6).

How can prudent partiers now say it's okay to drink in moderation?

I want to say this in a way that is understandable to you.

My wife and I love our children. They are the most precious gifts God has given to us outside of eternal life. As a couple, we have purposed in our hearts to do everything in our power to show them the character of Christ in all that we do. Sometimes we fall short, but God is faithful to help us past our limitations. But can I expect God to continually pick up the pieces for our family when I deliberately fail? I believe to have alcohol in my house or to drink socially at a dinner party is to dare God to keep my children in spite of my willful failure.

Life is too short, and the stakes are far too high to risk offending those around us. Self-indulgence in this matter in an effort to prove that "I can drink and still be a powerful Christian" is rather foolish in light of eternity.

The people we influence daily must see a clear and shining example of the purity and compassion of Christ. In our daily lives, they must see that we are practicing Paul's admonishment, ''And be not drunk with wine, wherein is excess; but be filled with the Spirit'' (Ephesians 5:18).

Dancing With The Devil

I love to have fun. But I like to see fun being enjoyed in a wholesome atmosphere. Some people think dancing is fun, but I personally believe that the dance is sensual and sexual in nature.

Young people and their parents often get upset with me when I talk about dancing. But before you stop reading, let me explain why.

A father verbally attacked me once for taking a stand against dancing. He said, ''I cannot believe that you stood in front of a group of young people in a church and took time to speak against dancing. I personally think there is nothing wrong with it. I have a wonderful, precious sixteen-year-old angel in my home, and we let her go to dances all the time. We see nothing wrong with it. We think it is a great place to meet friends and a great place to exercise.''

I thought that was funny. I said, ''Well, sir, I'm not trying to tell you what to do as a father. But I'm going to ask you, would you be willing to go with your sixteen-year-old to the next dance?''

''You better believe I will,'' he said and huffed off.

A couple of days later I got a call from this father. He was very apologetic and subdued this time. He said, "Rich, I want to apologize for attacking you in the area of the dance. I took your challenge and went with my daughter.

"We walked into the gymnasium where she met her boyfriend. When my little angel walked onto that dance floor, her halo fell off. The lights went out, the strobe lights came on, and the acid music began. In a matter of seconds, my little angel was changed into this writhing sex goddess who went through these incredible contortions in front of her boyfriend while he proceeded to dance all over his tongue.

"I almost started crying. But instead I ran onto the floor, grabbed my daughter, and marched her out of that dance hall. I decided I loved my girl too much to allow her to be placed into a compromising situation that she could not handle."

According to *CBS Reports,* over two thousand young women become pregnant every Friday night in America. If two thousand young women are becoming pregnant, how many more are having sex? And, why is this a Friday night statistic?

I feel it is because they have been out partying. When young people leave the dance or the neighborhood party where the music has been going, they are in a sensual frenzy. Those young people leave saying, "Forget the hamburgers, let's head for the lake." They are driven out of their minds sensually. Before they stop to think about what they're doing, they've become involved in an activity that breaks the heart of God.

A young man once came to me and said, "Rich, I don't see anything wrong with dancing."

I said, "Listen, if you can dance for five minutes with your girlfriend and not get turned on sexually, somebody ought to dig a six-foot hole, throw you in it, and cover you up because you're dead already." The dance is sexual and sensual.

Consider The Source

Where did the dance originate?

I believe it had its origin in the ancient heathen "phallic worship." Some theologians believe that when Moses came down from Mt. Sinai with the law of God in his hands, the children of Israel were involved in a wild, sensual dance unto the golden calf. The heathen dance began by raising the image of a male sex organ high into the air, and the people worshipped this symbol by dancing themselves into a sensual frenzy. Eventually, everyone found themselves a partner and had sex.

It's not much different on today's dance floors.

Some have said to me, "Rich Wilkerson, you are getting old. You don't know what is going on. You are not with it. We can handle this because we are liberated and 'prudent partiers.' We dance only in moderation."

How far is too far when people have put themselves into such compromising situations?

Every God-fearing Christian must come to terms with this *last-day* party mentality. I have little doubt that this partying lifestyle that has crept into the church is a sign of the end times. Jesus said in Matthew 24:37-38, "But as the days of Noah were, so shall also the Son of man be. For as in the days that were before the flood they were eating and drinking, and marrying and giving in marriage."

Those verses speak of a continual party. Today young people repeat a familiar phrase: "Drugs, sex, and rock 'n roll." Oddly enough those three words that spell P-A-R-T-Y to today's young adults were spoken of thousands of years ago by God through His prophet Hosea. The Living Bible says in Hosea 4:11, "Wine [drugs], women [sex], and song [rock 'n roll] have robbed my people of their brains."

Think of it! God is saying that His people have shelved their brains for a few fleeting moments of self-gratification. I ask you, Christian friend, are you willing to exchange eternity with God for seventy short, selfish turns around the sun?

Paul said in Galatians 2:20, "I am crucified with Christ: nevertheless I live; yet not I, but Christ liveth in me: and the life which I now live in the flesh I live by the faith of the Son of God, who loved me, and gave himself for me."

God called His Church to be *in* the world but not *of* the world. He didn't tell us to look strange, to dress weird, or be unaware of what is happening. He has called us to be alert, involved, and making an impact on our society. We can do that with the help of Christ living in us.

Chapter 3

FRUITFUL FORNICATION

Abortion is *not* our nation's number one problem: Our problem is *fornication*. Fornication is sexual intercourse between people who are not married.

When it comes to sexuality, Americans have made a mockery out of God's Word. Love has turned to lust; spirituality has been turned into sensuality; pious living is out and promiscuous living is in. There is little praying and much more parking. The marriage bedroom has been exchanged for the one-hour, no-tell motel room. Where we once believed in leaving and cleaving, people now cleave and usually leave.

God has given us this beautiful act of marriage to parallel His desire for intimate communion—obviously not in a physical way but in a spiritual way. He desires the kind of intimate communion with His Body, the Church, that a husband and wife enjoy in holy marriage.

When this beautiful act of love is spread around with anyone who moves, confusion sets in regarding our earthly partners. I believe we also receive a distorted image of God because of fornication. Let me tell you why.

The Mystical Maze

In the late 1960's, America experienced the beginning of a sexual revolution. The haven for free love revolved around the Haight-Ashbury hippie movement in San Francisco. Moral standards were thrown out the window. Absolutes were traded for experiential living.

During that period, young people lived together, traded sexual partners, and engaged in street orgies. Woodstock became the status symbol for the free love movement.

Along with this sexual freedom ran a parallel race toward cults and Eastern religions. Mystical, transcendental thoughts floated through the airways in the hippie music. The Beatles' movie and album, *Magical Mystery Tour,* promoted drugs and psychedelic experiences.

As young people got more "in touch" with themselves, they became more and more "out of touch" with God. The search was on to find deeper more wonderful experiences than anyone had known before. The Hare Krishnas, the Moonies, and other "love-is-the-answer" groups brainwashed our nation's children. Over four thousand of those cults still exist in this country, excluding the Jehovah's Witnesses and the Mormon Church.

Is The Pendulum Swinging?

If television is any indication of America's values, the swing, at least at the time of this writing, seems to be back toward the nuclear family. Dad has become the head of the family rather than the object of ridicule, and the dining room table has once again become the family counseling center.

Unfortunately, what has lingered from the sexual revolution is the fashionable thought that to engage in sex outside of mariage is okay. Television, movies, teen magazines, women's magazines, soap operas and yuppie-aged public school teachers (in many cases) have all added to this belief.

The Swingin' Singles

Recent statistics tell us that 48 percent of America's adults are single. That's a lot of unmarried adults!

God has created us to be social people. He has also created us with sexual appetites. What happens when those two needs are not met?

One new phenomena on the social scene is the singles' bar. I wish a neon sign could be placed in front of these bars that reads, "Come On In And Find Directions To Eternal Damnation." The singles' bar promises to satisfy those social needs with fun, fellowship, and fulfillment. But in reality what it offers is seductive, sexual situations that encourage sin. Believing that fulfillment can be found in one of these places is a lie straight from the pit of hell.

When does this Swingin' Singles philosophy begin?

I believe it begins as early as junior high school. Sometimes when I am ministering to young adults, I hand out a survey to the audience. People are honest when they don't have to sign their name. Their answers have astounded me. One out of five girls in this country has had intercourse before the age of thirteen. Over 70 percent of all senior guys have had sexual intercourse by the time they graduate from high school.

Growing up with that mentality, young people step out of school and into the singles' bar scene with little or no shock over fornication. It's the old story, "Well, everyone's doing it."

Christian singles have asked the question, "Well, Rich, what if I want to go to these places just to meet new people? My intentions are not immoral, but I enjoy meeting other singles."

I can only answer as Paul did: "I have written unto you not to keep company, if any man that is called a brother be a fornicator" (1 Corinthians 5:11).

Money Back Guarantee

The next step after the singles' bar is for a couple to move in together. The reason many of these couples choose living together over marriage is their own fear of failure. "Let's try it out and see if we like it first," they say.

That's like the man who lived next to a dairy farm. He said, "Why buy the cow when I can get my milk free?"

This is crazy. It reminds me of the little kid who went to the corner store to buy a popsicle. When he got there, he went straight to the freezer, pulled out a cherry popsicle, tasted it, and put the wrapper back on. "I changed my mind," he said. "I'd rather have grape." Once this kid has experienced and tasted that popsicle, there is no way he can put the wrapper back on and pick another one. You simply cannot taste popsicles before you buy them.

It is just as impossible for couples to "see if we like it first" before trying out marriage. When a person gives his body to another, God says it is for keeps!

The Bible says, "What? Know ye not that he which is joined to a harlot is one body? for two, saith he, shall be one flesh" (1 Corinthians 6:16).

Think of the "spiritual unions" that are taking place through illicit "love affairs" only to be trashed for the next *looker* who walks by. All of this illicit sowing is reaping a harvest of emotional and physical pain.

What Happened To The Absolutes?

Promiscuous living carries its own consequences. One is the rampant spread of sexual disease in the nation, and the other is unwanted pregnancy. God has His checks and balances when people refuse to take an absolute stand.

"Know ye not that the unrighteous shall not inherit the kingdom of God? Be not deceived: neither fornicators, nor idolaters, nor adulterers, nor effeminate, nor abusers of themselves with mankind, nor thieves, nor covetous, nor drunkards, nor revilers, nor extortioners, shall inherit the kingdom of God" (1 Corinthians 6:9-10).

When I was about eight years old, my father and I were standing with a group of men and one was telling a joke. In the punchline was the one-word answer "sex." It surprised me because I had never heard the word mentioned out loud before. Several of the men chuckled, and my dad turned red and walked away. That was the normal response twenty-five years ago.

Today, it's not unusual to go into a Christian bookstore and find books vividly describing sexual techniques for the marriage bed. My point is that we have come a long way from blushing at the word *sex*.

Someone once said, "What one generation condones, the next generation will openly practice."

Why is there a lack of absolute living? In the Old Testament there are two terms for God's statutes. They are—God's law and God's norm. In other words, God's law was normal. It was absolute. The Hebrew nation thought if you wanted to be normal, you had to live by God's law.

Later on, the Greeks introduced a word which developed a new way of thinking. This word was *ethos* which means "ethics." Ethics refers to the manner of life or conduct. But ethics change from generation to generation. Somewhere along the line, society changed God's law to man's ethics. Finite man will always water down the law.

For example, listen to the laws for church attendance in Jamestown, the first English settlement in the United States.

If a person missed church once, they lost one day's food rations. If they missed church a second time, they received a whipping with a horsewhip in the center of town. If they missed church a third time, they were placed in stockades for six months.

This had nothing to do with whether a person was a Christian or not. These were community laws. If you were a member of that community, you had to go to church.

Today, nearly four hundred years later, my home state of Washington boasts the poorest church attendance in the United States with less than 3 percent attending church on Sunday.

The pendulum has swung from extreme to extreme. But it's plain that the early settlers believed the power of God's Word would combat sin. Today, man's ethics say, "Let's be more reasonable in our thinking." Consequently, man's way has produced child abuse, wife-beating, incest, homosexuality, lesbianism, and every form of sexual filth one can imagine.

Invasion Of The Church

I know of a youth minister who has been imprisoned for having sex with several girls in his youth group. He was charged with statutory rape. I also know of a pastor who kept getting involved

46

sexually with the women in his church. His board kept forgiving him until they found out that he made one of the women he got pregnant get an abortion.

A young couple came to me several years ago who wanted to know my thoughts on premarital sex. They said, "We've been having oral sex for six months because our parents encouraged it. They thought it would be wrong to have intercourse because that was a sin against God." They were both seventeen years old.

I also knew a man who had been married for twelve years. This was his second marriage which produced two children. He was an usher in his church. One day this man walked into the house and said to his wife, "I'll be moving out tomorrow, and this is my last night here. I'm filing for divorce, and I'll be married the day the divorce is final. I'm living with a woman here in town." Within months the divorce was finalized. This man is now remarried and back in the same pew in the balcony, raising his hands and praising the Lord, as though nothing had happened.

God has not called us to follow Him when it is convenient or when it fits in with the current social thinking. Great fruit cannot come from immoral living.

The apostle Paul left no gray areas and no room for carnal thinking regarding the single or married Christian. He addressed the fornication issue in 1 Corinthians 5, 6, and 7.

The "party mentality" within the church does not help God's message of holiness and purity but rather hinders the work of grace in a person's life.

Is There A Solution?

Fornication is sin. Those who commit this sin are on their way to hell unless they repent and receive forgiveness from God. "Having therefore these promises, dearly beloved, let us cleanse ourselves from all filthiness of the flesh and spirit, perfecting holiness in the fear of God" (2 Corinthians 7:1).

How often have you heard the message of holiness and purity preached? Whether it is popular or not, the truth must be told. God's law is absolute regardless of what society thinks. If all society becomes reprobate and only one man stays righteous before God, that one man is normal and all of society is abnormal.

It's time to return to the law of the absolutes. "Wives, submit yourselves unto your own husbands, as unto the Lord. For the husband is the head of the wife, even as Christ is the head of the church.... Husbands, love your wives, even as Christ also loved the church ... and they two shall be one flesh. This is a great mystery: but I speak concerning Christ and the church" (Ephesians 5:22-23,25,31-32).

Christ has paralleled the sexual union in marriage with His relationship with the Church.

I believe there are professing Christians involved in sexual sin who, if they died right now, would end up in hell believing God had led them there. They've justified their sin for so long that they

48

believe God has condoned it. But God's law never changes.

What is the answer then? God gave it to us long ago. "Now the body is not for fornication, but for the Lord" (1 Corinthians 6:13). "Flee fornication. Every sin that a man doeth is without the body; but he that committeth fornication sinneth against his own body" (1 Corinthians 6:18).

To those who have had many sexual partners, I want you to know the Word of God is true. God forbids fornication. If shame and guilt flood your heart at this point, listen to what God says, "Now we know that God's judgment against those who do such things is based on truth. So when you, a mere man, pass judgment on them and yet do the same things, do you think you will escape God's judgment? Or do you show contempt for the riches of his kindness, tolerance and patience, not realizing that God's kindness leads you toward repentance?" (Romans 2:2-4 *NIV).*

God will deal justly with sin; however, it's His goodness and mercy that drives us to repentance. He does not want to emphasize His harshness but rather His goodness in granting us another chance. God's desire is to free us from sin and shame.

After repentance, we must develop a heart after God. Listen to the cry of God's heart in Deuteronomy 5:29: "O that there were such an heart in them, that they would fear me, and keep all my commandments always, that it might be well with them, and with their children forever!" Our God does not want to hit us over the head with legalistic meanness, but rather He wants our lives to go well.

We also need a "washing of regeneration, and renewing of the Holy Ghost" (Titus 3:5). This nation is reeling from an overdose of sexual fantasies and promiscuities. Billboards, television shows, advertisements, rock songs, and men's heroes are all propagating sex, sex, sex. We need a perfect, spiritual washing of God's Word to counteract all of Satan's trash.

Once we begin to thirst after God, He will begin to meet the desires of our heart. It won't be abortion, abortion, abortion or sex, sex, sex, but rather gracious Father, precious Jesus, blessed Holy Spirit.

We need Christian men and women who will live and preach absolutely, no matter what the ethics of their day say. We, in the church, must become the light of the world—the torchbearers.

Jeremiah looked in the face of the most respected prophet of his day, Hananiah, and called him a liar. It wasn't the ethical thing to do, but God's ways are not man's ways.

In Luke 9:51, Jesus "stedfastly set his face to go to Jerusalem." He was absolute in His direction. He knew what it was going to cost Him, but He made up His mind to do it.

David said in Psalm 108:1, "O God, my heart is fixed. I will sing and give praise." He had made up his mind.

Paul said in Philippians 1:17, "I am set for the defence of the gospel." He was talking about living and preaching absolutely.

The Church must preach the absolute authority of the Scriptures and the absolute Lordship of

Jesus Christ. We must preach and live the absolute imminent return of Christ. When we do, we will not grow lax and weak in the area of sexual immorality.

Jesus said in Matthew 12:30, "He that is not with me is against me; and he that gathereth not with me scattereth abroad." In other words, you are either lost or saved. There is no middle road.

The Bible is God's Word—it doesn't "contain" God's Word.

If people would live according to God's Word, they would have double miracles rather than double standards. What the devil meant for evil, God can turn around for good. God can turn a miserable failure into a miracle.

When people say, "Well, if I wouldn't have committed this sin, I would have never learned this lesson." I think if they had never committed that sin, they would still have learned God's principles and many others. Sin starts the walk backward, causing a person to lose valuable time in his walk with God.

God will teach us what we need to know, when we need to know it. I believe if we will live according to His law, God will give us experience and opportunity far beyond what our age says we should have experienced.

Chapter 4

DIVINE DIVORCE

Several years ago, I conducted a funeral for a man who was living with a common-law wife. It was crazy. The dead man's common-law wife had kept the name of the last husband to whom she had been legally married. Her two sons, who had called this man in the casket their father, had different last names from each other and different from their mother. Each had been fathered by a different man from the mother's previous marriages. The mother of the dead man was divorced, and her last name wasn't the same as her son's. Also attending the funeral were the parents of the common-law wife—and they had a different name, of course. You can imagine how comical this scene was.

As I left the funeral home that day, I thought how common divorce, remarriage, half-brothers, half-sisters, stepmoms, and stepdads had become. What is even harder to comprehend is that this mixed-up scene is becoming part of the ''Christian'' community.

Many times when I speak at a youth convention,

I invite those from broken homes to come to the altar to pray that God will heal their wounds. One-third of the congregation usually comes. At a recent convention, kids streamed to the altar, many of them crying. I watched a pastor turn around and kneel by his chair, weeping uncontrollably. He told me later, "I knew problems existed with divorce in the world; but when I saw those hundreds of Christian kids from broken homes come down the aisles, I couldn't believe it. It just took me by surprise."

A couple, who attended a church where I was speaking, tried to persuade me that God had led them to divorce their mates and marry each other. "We prayed about it, and God told us to divorce," they insisted. "We praise His name because it has made our lives so much better."

Divorce has moved into the church with alarming statistics. A leading radio minister reports that 38 percent of all evangelicals are ending their marriages.

How can this be possible? Maybe our lack of absolute teaching is again the culprit.

Billy Graham has said, "I am opposed to divorce and regard the increase in divorce today as one of the most alarming problems in society. However, I know that the Lord can forgive and heal even when great sin may have been involved. The Church is made up of sinners."

As a minister, I have had the opportunity to join many young couples in holy matrimony. I try to tell them the importance of the contract they are entering into. Too often they are in such a state of infatuation that they don't hear.

I'm convinced that few couples really pay attention to the vows they make. The minister says, "Will you take this person to be your wedded spouse? Will you live together according to God's law concerning marriage? Will you love, comfort, honor, and keep him or her in sickness and in health? Will you forget and leave all others behind and keep yourself only for this individual as long as both of you are alive?" To all the questions, they answer, "I WILL."

Out of one hundred couples in America, fifty-five of them tell a lie before God and man while standing at the holy altar. Where is the perseverance, the stamina, the determination to stay together?

Oh, For Greener Pastures

When a person believes that Mrs. Brown's or Mr. Smith's backyard has "greener grass," he or she has already been deceived. Happiness cannot be found next door, down the street, or in another city. Happiness cannot be found by exchanging problems.

Listen to what Helen Hosier said in her book, *The Other Side of Divorce,* "Divorce is not a solution. It is not the answer that automatically insures the one seeking divorce is going to live happily ever after. Divorce is not easy. It is tough and unpleasant. It is difficult to discuss and even more difficult for me to write about. Divorce is hurtful to many people, not just the ones involved in the divorce action. It is hurtful to the cause of Christ. Divorce is ugly—ugly to onlookers, ugly to those who can only surmise the whys and wherefores, ugly to children, ugly to those most affected—the man and woman. Divorce is costly, financially, emotionally, physically, spiritually.... Divorce is painful. It is a chaotic time. A time of sadness, struggle, anguish, anxiety and trauma. Count on it, you will shed some tears if you are at all sensitive—this includes men as well as women.''[1]

This sure doesn't sound as though going through a divorce is much fun.

Jesus recognized the problem of divorce. He knew the divorced person would one day expect to marry again. In doing so, Jesus said, they would commit adultery and cause the new partner to commit adultery. Adultery is sexual activity involving at least one married person outside the marriage boundary. That is why Jesus wanted to prevent divorce.

But He did add an exception in Matthew 5:32. ''But I say unto you, That whosoever shall put away his wife, saving for the cause of fornication, causeth her to commit adultery: and whosoever shall marry her that is divorced committeth adultery.''

An exception is also stated in 1 Corinthians 7:15. ''But if the unbelieving depart, let him depart. A brother or a sister is not under bondage in such cases: but God hath called us to peace.''

If Only I Could Go Back

I have a dear friend whose parents divorced after nearly thirty years of marriage. After all those years and raising six children all whom now serve God, this man's mother decided to divorce his father. She cited irreconcilable differences. The entire family was shocked. Now, years later, my friend's father has remarried, but his mother is struggling to pick up the pieces of her life.

Recently she told my friend, "You know, Son, your dad was a pretty good guy. He took care of us and was loyal to us. I just chose to focus in on his negative points. If I could only go back and do it again, I know I would find that the positive far outweighed the negative."

Some of you reading this book may feel like that woman did—'If only I could go back." But you can't. And I do not intend to inflict guilt and remorse over what might have been. *There is no condemnation in Christ!* (See Romans 8:1.) God will help put the pieces of your life back together again; and, in many cases, He already has.

I am, however, very concerned for the one who is now contemplating divorce. What did you mean when you stood at the altar and said "for better or for worse"? It is so important to ask God today to show you the far-reaching implications of the decision you are about to make. As much as you detest your spouse, is it possible that in five years you may say, "If only I could go back and do it again"?

What Does God Say About Divorce?

Marriage is a basic human relationship ordained by God. (See Genesis 1:27 and 2:18.) God intended marriage to be a lifelong, monogamous union. (See Genesis 2:24; Matthew 19:5-6; and Mark 10:6-9.) Marriage is a solemn binding agreement made between God and man.

God hates divorce.

"Because the Lord hath been witness between thee and the wife of thy youth, against whom thou hast dealt treacherously: yet is she thy companion and the wife of thy covenant. And did not he make one? Yet had he the residue of the spirit. And wherefore one? That he might seek a godly seed. Therefore take heed to your spirit, and let none deal treacherously against the wife of his youth. For the Lord, the God of Israel, saith that he hateth putting away" (Malachi 2:14-16).

God said divorce is treachery against your companion. It is also a violent act coming from a wrong spirit. "What therefore God hath joined together, let not man put asunder" (Matthew 19:6). Therefore, divorce is not God's original intention for man.

Jesus told us that divorce is contrary to God's perfect will. Paul reminded us again, "And unto the married I command, yet not I, but the Lord, Let not the wife depart from her husband: But and if she depart, let her remain unmarried, or be reconciled to her husband: and let not the husband put away his wife" (1 Corinthians 7:10-12).

Paul also forbids Christians to take the initiative

in getting a divorce because their partner is an unbeliever. (See 1 Corinthians 7:12-16.) God spelled out His Word clearly. A person cannot be confused who chooses to follow God's Word.

John MacArthur says:

> If there is confusion about the subject of divorce and remarriage, it is not because God has given us a confused word in Scripture. Rather, it is because rampant sin entering the world has confused the simplicity of what God has said.
>
> The confusion arises when we try to accomodate the divine standard to the lack of standards in our contemporary morality, or when we try to compensate for the low standards of society with a higher law than God set in His Word. Both are wrong approaches.[2]

From Ashes To Beauty

Happiness begins by having a relationship with Jesus Christ. If a Christian came to me contemplating a divorce, I would ask them first about their relationship with Jesus. Then I would ask them to account for any sin or bitterness. We are responsible to account for ourselves first. Anger and wrong attitudes may have contributed to the problem.

Next, I would encourage anyone contemplating leaving his or her spouse to begin reading the

Word of God. People who are considering a break-up are usually those who have not had time alone with the Lord. It's very difficult to have a continued life of peace and serenity within the marriage when you have no relationship with Christ.

I don't step out on my wife because I have a relationship with her based upon intimate communion. We love each other. We communicate. When I'm on the road, I phone home every night. We cannot have this intimate relationship without communicating with each other. But many Christians are Christians in name only. They have no relationship with Christ. They don't know the Word of God.

The Word of God is His main means of communication to His people. But if His people are not reading it, you can be sure little relationship with Him exists.

Those struggling in a marriage are often struggling in their relationship with the Lord also. They're trying to do it all by themselves. The Bible says, "Casting all your care upon him: for he careth for you" (1 Peter 5:7). If we are not willing to study the Word of God, pray, and seek His face, it stands to reason that we'll run into problems with our mate. Those problems aren't going to go away on their own. A Christian must develop a relationship with Christ now.

I would also urge the person, either recently divorced or contemplating divorce, to get involved in a church. Becoming involved with caring Christians will sustain a couple through a difficult time. God can and does still work miracles.

About all we hear some Christians asking these days is, "How can I get out of this troubled relationship and still please God?" They want God's stamp of approval on their coming actions.

I've watched Christians in a troubled marriage purposely fall back from their Christian responsibilities. While in a state of rebellion, they divorce each other, find new marriage partners, ask God for forgiveness, and end up back in their church as though nothing ever happened.

This puts an incredible burden upon the church family. They are now supposed to accept the situation without hesitation. The children in the church are supposed to figure out what happened to their friend's mommy and daddy and justify it in their little minds with no questions asked.

Everyone is affected when one or both of the marriage partners is selfish. *Sin robs!*

I'm not making light of the marriage pact, but I thank God for husbands and wives who don't run when their spouse falls into sin. Hosea, a great man of God, had a prostitute for a wife! God commanded him, as an illustration of God's love for apostate Israel, to take back his beloved. Hosea forgave her and took her back.

When a spouse falls into temptation and sins, he or she is all too often cut off by his or her mate. Once again, it is imperative that we realize marriage to be a spiritual parallel to Christ's relationship with us. When I consider the continual grace God has in taking us back when we fall, I am amazed.

Think of the homes that could be salvaged if

forgiveness became the order of the day!

God is sovereignly against divorce! Divorce breaks His heart.

God does not lead anyone into divorce. He may allow us to go through struggles, but victory should always be the end result.

"No temptation has seized you except what is common to man. And God is faithful; he will not let you be tempted beyond what you can bear. But when you are tempted, he will also provide a way out so that you can stand up under it" (1 Corinthians 10:13 *NIV*).

Chapter 5

PRECIOUS PRIDE

Throughout this book, I have been discussing the problem of Christians who live in a worldly manner. In this chapter, I want to talk about pride. Again, the words *precious* and *pride* do not go together. Pride is not precious in God's sight. Yet the church is reeling with pride.

Jesus said in Matthew 16:24, "If any man will come after me, let him deny himself, and take up his cross, and follow me."

In 1 Corinthians 1:27-29, the Bible says, "But God hath chosen the foolish things of the world to confound the wise; and God hath chosen the weak things of the world to confound the things which are mighty; and base things of the world, and things which are despised, hath God chosen, yea, and things which are not, to bring to nought things that are: That no flesh should glory in his presence."

Paul said in Galatians 6:14, "God forbid that I should glory, save in the cross of our Lord Jesus Christ."

So why then has humanistic psychology

permeated the Church of Christ? One of the main reasons is the same one the world uses. Pride says, "You've got to stand up for your own rights."

What is pride? Winkie Pratney writes, "Pride is thinking we can act apart from God. It is saying we don't need Him in all we do. It is acting as if no one in the universe is more important than us. But basically it is simply the refusal to acknowledge that we are what we actually are in the eyes of God."[1]

One of the saddest stories in the Bible is about a man named Jonah and his rights. Jonah had a problem with pride. God told Jonah to go to the city of Ninevah and cry against them because of their sin. But Jonah rebelled. After all, he had a right to say "no," didn't he?

Instead of obeying God, Jonah went to Tarshish on a ship. Enroute to Tarshish, a storm came up and Jonah was thrown overboard and swallowed by a whale. But God in His mercy delivered Jonah. God tried again by saying to Jonah, "Arise, go unto Ninevah, that great city, and preach unto it the preaching that I bid thee" (Jonah 3:2).

Coerced, Jonah went to Ninevah unrepentant in his rebellion. Jonah cried, "Yet forty days, and Ninevah shall be overthrown," just as God had told him to.

The people of Ninevah believed God and repented.

"But it displeased Jonah exceedingly, and he was very angry" (Jonah 4:1). Paraphrased, Jonah said to God, "Listen, when You asked me to go and say 'In forty days this town is going to perish,' I knew that if they repented You would forget it and forgive them—and that is exactly what You did. And it made me look bad."

Jonah wanted to stand up for his rights. He told Ninevah that God would overthrow the city, and that's what he wanted God to do. Pride had overwhelmed this man.

A lot of "Christian" people are in the same boat today. They don't want to lose face. They want to hold onto their rights. But God wants us to lay them down. "If any man will come after me, let him deny himself, and take up his cross, and follow me" (Luke 9:23).

Looking Out For Number One

Another strong emphasis that exists in the church today is ... *looking out for number one*. "Watch out for yourself because no one will fight for you. You are on your own."

I believe much error exists in the church because Christian men and women are going ahead without checking with the Lord or receiving counsel from others. God has designed us to be a "body" of believers, working and functioning together. (See 1 Corinthians 12 and 14.)

The Bible says that when one member of the Body suffers, all the members suffer. If one has a need, everyone experiences that need. "Bear ye one another's burdens, and so fulfil the law of Christ. For if a man think himself to be something, when he is nothing, he deceiveth himself" (Galatians 6:2-3).

In his book, *The Normal Christian Life,* Watchman Nee says: "If we give ourselves unreservedly to God, many adjustments may have to be made: in family, or business, or Church relationships, or in the matter of our personal views. God will not let anything of ourselves remain. His finger will touch, point by point, everything that is not of Him, and will say: 'this must go.' Are you willing? It is foolish to resist God, and always wise to submit to Him. We admit that many of us still have controversy with the Lord. He wants something, while we want something else. Many things we dare not look into, dare not pray about, dare not even think about, lest we lose our peace. We can evade the issue in that way but to do so will bring us out of the will of God. It is always an easy matter to get out of His will, but it is a blessed thing just to hand ourselves over to him and let Him have His way with us."[2]

Democracy In The Church

The New Testament church was not a democracy. God never intended the church to operate as one. Today people are being elected and appointed, however, to deacon and pastoral positions by means of a popular vote. God cares nothing about popularity.

God knows who He wants to fill a position. We can vote all we want; but if it is not the will of God, God will write "Ichabod" across the top of the doorpost.

I know pastors who live in fear because their

three-year-vote is ready to come before the congregation. They are not free to preach what they feel God wants them to preach because it may step on the toes of Mr. Committee Head.

Pride-oriented people stand as much against God as Jonah did.

Read Acts 12 if you want to see a good example of pride. One day Herod, dressed in royal apparel, sat on his throne and addressed the people. In verse 22, they said, "It is the voice of a god, and not of a man." Herod took all the glory for himself, and God sent worms to eat his body.

Some Christians need to check for worms.

Overwhelmed by pride and arrogance, they think others should pay much attention to them. Let me share with you two valuable lessons God taught me about pride.

Learning The Way Of Humility

In my second year of seminary, I traveled with a singing group made up of five young men. We represented our school for two months, performing sixty concerts in fifty-two nights, and traveling 12,000 miles through fourteen states.

During that time, we sang the same songs and gave the same speeches between the songs for two straight months, every night, sometimes twice a day. We had little Bible study, if any, among us. Before we went on the platform for the evening meeting, we would say a short prayer.

Working on this schedule made us tired and cranky, and we soon became critical of everything and everyone. We even became critical of each other, until all five of us ended up hating each other and ourselves.

When the two-month tour was over, I went home for one Sunday. My father was the pastor of our church in Minneapolis. That Sunday I sat next to a very close friend of our family. Guests had been invited that day to lead the service. Since criticism had become second nature to me, I sat there cutting down these people one after another to our family friend. I would make a joke or be cynical or laugh. This man was a kind and fun-loving person, and I thought I was amusing him.

But, at the end of the service, this man said, "Rich, could I talk to you before you leave?" So we headed down to the church prayer room where he got us both a chair. As we sat facing each other, I cracked more jokes thinking this would be a light session. Then I noticed he was crying. I said, "What's wrong?"

"Well, Rich," he said, "I love you and I love your parents. But I have to tell you something, and I don't want to because it may mean the end of a friendship. But I love you too much not to tell you. You have developed a critical spirit. For a young man, you are filled with pride. Rich, if you don't take care of this, you won't have any impact as a minister. People will pick up on this pride and arrogance and won't want to have anything to do with you. You'll be a failure, Rich."

Then it was my turn to cry. That Sunday afternoon the two of us knelt together, and I repented before God. That godly man started me out in the ministry by having the courage to confront me.

On The Road To Kalispell

Another time that God dealt with me about pride was while I was on my way to Kalispell, Montana to speak to about three thousand young people at a high school assembly. I headed out into a cold, dark morning to catch a 7:00 a.m. flight. After parking in the budget lot, throwing bags and boxes onto the bus, and working up a sweat in the cold morning air, I finally checked in at 6:30 a.m. onto the Northwest flight. Imagine doing all this just to get to Kalispell.

As I settled into my seat, I heard the captain say there would be a one-hour delay because fog had just rolled in. What? A one-hour delay? That one-hour delay would be just long enough for me to miss my connecting flight to Kalispell from Spokane. I thought, God, what about the kids? What about all the planning?

I sat in the Spokane airport restaurant wondering what to do. The assembly had to be cancelled. Barring any other problems, I could still arrive in Kalispell late that afternoon to speak at the evening rally. But without the school assembly and having to compete with Monday Night Football on television, I thought the evening crowd would look like a small gathering of the ladies sewing guild.

This trip to Kalispell was not turning out the way I had planned. "Why, God?" I asked. Why did the fog roll in this morning? Why did You let this happen? Who knows when I'll ever get back to Kalispell again?

Here were some of my logical conclusions: Maybe Kalispell is a different place. Maybe they don't have drug problems there like the rest of the country. Maybe Kalispell has no problems with drugs at all. Maybe all the young people detest alcohol in Kalispell. Maybe there are no problems with immorality in Kalispell. Even though more than half of all teenagers engage in sexual intercourse before they graduate from high school, maybe no one has ever polled Kalispell. Maybe these kids are the caring and committed type who aren't driven by their lusts and feelings. Maybe none of these kids are rebellious toward their parents. Maybe they all come from loving families where peace reigns. Maybe they respect authority in Kalispell. Maybe the kids in that town hate rock music and spend their time memorizing Scriptures instead of rock lyrics. Maybe they all have a high level of self-esteem in Kalispell. Maybe no one in that town ever came close to thinking of suicide. Maybe they just don't need any kind of ministry in Kalispell. Maybe that is why God let the fog roll in.

Then I had this terrible thought that maybe God had given up on Kalispell. Maybe the folks were so bad there that God had lifted His Spirit from that city. I knew it is possible to reject God's promptings so much that He finally quits prompting you. Maybe that's what was going on in Kalispell. Maybe God has written the word Ichabod over the doorpost of that city. Maybe that is why God let the fog roll in.

The more I thought about the whole Kalispell thing, the more I felt like I was missing something. There had to be a key. No way could Kalispell be filled with perfect teenagers who don't need the gospel because they all love God. No way could that have been the case.

There was also no way that God had given up on that town. If God was going to repeat a Sodom and Gomorrah destructon, He was surely not going to start with Kalispell. I could think of at least twenty-five other cities that would have to go before Kalispell. It had to be something, something. What was it?

Then suddenly God revealed what it was. I couldn't believe it. Oh, Jesus, help me. *I was the problem.* The fog rolled in because of me! I had been pointing fingers all morning, but the finger was really pointing at me. I had been on a high horse lately, speaking to thousands of kids, gaining national recognition in some circles, and being responsible for a growing staff and a growing family. I had traveled worldwide, been on television, and written several books. My pride had overwhelmed me.

I sat at that restaurant table thinking I would write a message that would leave people talking about the power of God; but instead, God had revealed an old problem to me.

Trying not to weep in the presence of those near me, I searched the Scriptures and came to a familiar passage that had given me hope in the past. "But he said to me, 'My grace is sufficient for you, for my power is made perfect in weakness.' Therefore I will boast all the more gladly about my weaknesses, so that Christ's power may rest on me. That is why, for Christ's sake, I delight in weaknesses, in insults, in hardships, in persecutions, in difficulties. For when I am weak, then I am strong'' (2 Corinthians 12:9-10 *NIV*).

I needed the road to Kalispell that morning because God was working on me again. Thank God the fog rolled in! It helped to remind me that it is more important to know God than to know anyone else or do anything else.

Kids can spot a phony whether it is in Kalispell or in Kalamazoo.

Having A Servant's Heart

Jim Elliot was a missionary and a man who had a heart after God. His wife Elisabeth has published part of his journal. On January 16, 1950, Jim wrote, ''Deserted all morning. Much time on my knees but no fervency or any desire for prayer. No heed or harkening in study of the Word either. What good is Greek, commentaries, insight, gifts, and all the rest if there is no heart for Christ? Oh, what slackness I feel in me now. Wasted half a day.''[3]

What good is Greek, commentaries, insight, gifts and all the rest if there is no heart for Christ? I guess that's what it's all about—this thing of pride.

In David Brainerd's personal journal, he says, ''As I walked out this morning to the same place as I was last night, I began to find it sweet to pray and think of undergoing the greatest sufferings for the cause of Christ with pleasure and found myself willing, if God should so order it, to suffer banishment from my native land among the heathen that I might do something for their salvation and distresses and deaths of any kind. God gave me to wrestle earnestly for others, for the kingdom of Christ in the world and for dear Christian friends. I felt weaned from the world, from my own reputation amongst men. Willing to be despised and to be a gazing stock for the world to behold."[4]

That's what happens when a person yields to Christ as opposed to remaining full of pride. This generation's god seems to be tied in with that slogan—"I've got my pride."

Solomon said in Proverbs 16:18, "Pride goeth before destruction, and an haughty spirit before a fall." He also said in Proverbs 29:23, "A man's pride shall bring him low." Oh, if we could only yield to Christ.

Pride has split churches, divided homes, and cost men their positions.

But God is calling Christians to servanthood.

Paul opens many of his letters with, "Paul, a servant of Jesus Christ, called to be an apostle, separated unto the gospel of God, a servant of Jesus Christ."

To Titus, he wrote, "Paul, a servant of God." To Philemon, he wrote, "Paul, a prisoner of Jesus Christ." His love for God was powerful. Paul wanted only to serve Christ.

I know a pastor who has a lead helper named Bill. Several years ago this pastor received a death threat one Sunday morning in the offering plate. The note said that in the coming days there would be a bomb placed in the pastor's car and he would be killed.

After the service that day, the pastor came into the office and was told what the note said. He replied, "Well, God will protect me. I'm God's servant. However God wants to, He can take care of me." As he walked through the door of his office to leave, Bill took the keys from the pastor's hand and said, "Pastor, beginning today, I'll be starting your car. This town could easily get along without me, but this town could never get along without you."

That was over two years ago, and Bill is still starting the pastor's car.

You see, God is not looking for stars. He's just looking for people to humble themselves.

My Grandma Holloway passed away in 1983. She was 83 years old. She didn't leave me any money. She had very little of that; although she never had to look our way for any financial support. She didn't leave me any of Grandad's books; they had all been snatched up long before Grandma's death.

She told my mother to give me her own Bible. It was the greatest thing that Grandma could have left me. I was looking through it the other day. In the back of her Bible I came across a prayer that she had written in the hospital in 1954, after my granddad had his fatal stroke. She was all alone in the room that night.

It seems appropriate to conclude this chapter on pride with Grandma's prayer.

A Prayer From My Heart
by Grandma Holloway

What does it mean I ask, dear Lord,
To love You with all my heart?
To love You with all my soul, my strength?
This knowledge to me impart.
Our love can never reach the height,
Nor fathom love like Thine;
But let my life, I pray, dear Lord,
Fit in Thy great design.
All that I have, I give Thee, Lord,
My all on the altar lay.
Burn up the dross, show me Thy cross,
And take all of self away.

Chapter 6

RIGHTEOUS REBELS

I've been in the ministry since 1972. I suppose the one thing that I've observed more than anything else in those years is that rebellion thwarts the plan of God. Righteous rebels are two words that really don't go together.

This problem of rebellion follows closely on the heels of "spiritual pride." Jesus prayed in Matthew 6:10, "Thy kingdom come. Thy will be done in earth, as it is in heaven."

How is God's will done in heaven? I believe it is accomplished with no hindrance. There's no rebellion in heaven. Jesus knew from personal experience how peaceful and serene and secure it was to live 24 hours a day in the perfect will of God. He longs for that same heavenly environment to come to earth. Too often, however, rebellion raises its ugly head and hinders the plan of God.

"Who Does He Think He Is?"

Rebellion is often cloaked with righteousness. A good example of this is in the story of Miriam,

Moses' sister. Miriam didn't like Moses' wife. She was so upset that she said to her other brother Aaron, "Hath the Lord indeed spoken only by Moses? Hath he not also spoken by us?" (Numbers 12:2). In other words, Miriam was saying, "Who does Moses think he is? Does Moses think he is the only one God can use? God can use us, too, Aaron."

Here is what I think happened in Miriam's life. I believe that Miriam had pride built up in her heart and failed to discern God's authority and God's leadership in God's man. When Israel marched across dry land to the other side of the Red Sea, Miriam was so excited that she danced for joy. (See Exodus 15:20-21.)

It was a spontaneous, righteous dance for joy, and it pleased God. Miriam was a spiritual woman, given to spiritual things. She was not light-hearted—but wise. As a little girl, she watched over Moses when he was in the bulrushes. Even in her youth, Miriam had spiritual wisdom.

But somewhere along the way, something changed. After crossing the Red Sea, people began to see Moses as their leader. As his leadership increased, so did Miriam's. But she failed to discern that people respected her because of her brother's leadership, not because she was an outstanding woman of God.

When I was a little kid, I was somewhat rebellious. The deacons in our church would pat me on the head and say, "Nice little Rich." I didn't realize it was because I was the pastor's son. Probably ten feet past me they thought, What a jerk.

78

I was loved out of respect for my father—their spiritual leader.

This is what happened to Miriam. As her popularity grew, she allowed pride to rule her thinking.

Do you remember when Jimmy Carter was president? At any other time in history, Billy Carter, the youngest brother, would never have made the news. But because his brother was the president, Billy received a lot of national attention. Along the way, old Billy thought he was somebody special.

Miriam also failed to understand that her brother was God's man. She kept seeing him as the little brother who still needed her help. Spiritual pride took over.

As a result, rebellion raised its ugly head, and Miriam lashed out against Moses. She touched the anointed one of God.

"And the anger of the Lord was kindled against them ... And the cloud departed from off the tabernacle; and, behold, Miriam became leprous, white as snow" (Numbers 12:9-10). The next time Miriam's name is mentioned it is in her obituary. What a sad indictment of a woman who loved the Lord but allowed pride and rebellion to rule in her life.

The Ground Opens Up

Another case of spiritual pride that moved into rebellion is found in Numbers 16. Korah, Dathan, and Abiram rose up against Moses.

As you read this story, equate it with a select

group of people within the church who get on their hobby horse, find a few other people in the church, and begin some stupid little thing against leadership. Maybe the pastor commissioned workers to paint the men's bathroom orange, and these people don't like orange. But they have found something to fight for—however unrighteous it may appear.

"And they rose up before Moses, with certain of the children of Israel, two hundred and fifty princes of the assembly, famous in the congregation, men of renown: And they gathered themselves together against Moses and against Aaron, and said unto them, Ye take too much upon you, seeing all the congregation are holy, every one of them, and the Lord is among them: wherefore then lift ye up yourselves above the congregation of the Lord?" (Numbers 16:2-3).

They said, "Who do you think you are? We are all men of God. God can use all of us." Korah was jealous.

But when Moses heard this, he fell on his face. He knew how God would respond to rebels. He knew that Korah, Dathan, and Abiram were asking for trouble.

Moses fell on his face before the Lord to plead their case. This is the difference between the loving leader and the "righteous rebel." These men were rebelling with righteous overtones.

If rebellion had not arisen within the camp, the tragedy that followed would never have happened. When the showdown came as to whom God had chosen as leader, "the ground clave asunder that was under them: And the earth opened her mouth, and swallowed them up, and their houses, and all the men that appertained unto Korah, and all their goods'' (Numbers 16:31-32).

God has given us more than we deserve, and we cannot take what He has not given. Sometimes, I believe, when things are going just great, certain people in the church long for some kind of controversy or some cause. It is not enough that people are getting saved at our altars every weekend, not enough that the preacher is anointed, and not enough that families are doing well. This is boring to some, so they stir things up.

Rebellion says, ''I want all this, and I want to be in charge, too.''

It is a terrible thing to face God's judgment. But I see more and more Christians willing to take that risk and step out in rebellion. They would rather face God than get off their little hobby horse.

A man stood against my grandfather for ten years. This man caused my grandfather's family no end of pain and suffering. One day while Grandfather was praying, God said, ''Go talk to the man and tell him that My patience is at an end. If he refuses to repent, he is going to be diseased and die.'' My grandfather went to this man and repeated what God had told him to say, but the man laughed in his face and all but cursed him. Within a month, that man was dead from cancer.

A friend of mine once pastored a church that rebelled against his leadership. After many years of serving that church, he was forced to leave because of some made-up stories. Several months after the pastor had resigned, the leader of that rebellion fell off a roof onto his head. That wealthy man was killed instantly.

I did not write this chapter to talk about God's judgment but rather about the tragedy of rebellion.

Rebellion cannot hide behind righteousness. Church schisms are becoming commonplace, and these splits are a terrible testimony to the world. Terrible! This testimony is like spitting in God's face. What the world sees is a church that can't work together or manage its affairs. It sees people who are always griping and complaining, hassling and arguing.

The church must wake up and see that the battle is outside, not inside, the church walls! As long as the devil can keep us fighting internally, he is assured that we'll never go out to fight where the war really is.

Yeah ... But!

Now let's look back at the life of King Saul. Saul started out with a heart for God. But cloaked in righteous thinking, he did what was right in his own eyes—he became a rebel. In 1 Samuel 15:3, God told Saul to "go and smite Amalek, and utterly destroy all that they have, and spare them not; but slay both man and woman, infant and suckling, ox and sheep, camel and ass."

Saul, however, thought he had a better idea than God did. "But Saul and the people spared Agag, and the best of the sheep, and of the oxen, and of the fatlings, and the lambs, and all that was good, and would not utterly destroy them" (1 Samuel 15:9). Saul's idea was to keep the good sheep and have plenty to sacrifice to God.

It's the old "yeah—but" principle. "Yeah—but I've got a better idea," says the rebel.

Saul's steps to destruction were lying, consulting a medium (witchcraft), and finally suicide.

Once a rebel has decided he has a better idea than God, he must raise himself up on his hobby horse and lie to cover up his rebellion. The result is a loss of anointing. Once the anointing is lost, the rebel must try to maintain his spirituality by using human ways and human reasonings.

Satan's lie to man has always been—you can be in charge of your own life and run it yourself. America is a rebel land full of rebellious people. Witchcraft has become a major problem in our cities. God's answer to Saul is the same answer given to us today. "Rebellion is as the sin of witchcraft" (1 Samuel 15:23).

A Word To A Rebel

Perhaps God has been talking over your bright future with Jesus and the Holy Spirit this week. While they have been talking about blessing you, you may be thinking about stirring up a little unrighteous commotion.

The children of Israel were like that. They were always winning, winning, winning ... until one day, they lost.

In the midst of all their spiritual blessing, Israel "began to commit whoredom with the daughters of Moab" (Numbers 25:1). Israel thought they had a better idea—a new form of worship. Twenty-four thousand people died as a result of that "better idea."

If twenty-four thousand people were killed in your city, imagine the sorrow, grief, and weeping it would create. You would think such a tragedy would have taken care of the rebellion in Israel. But it didn't!

Right in the midst of all this grief, a young man, drunk with lust, brought a Midianite woman into this broken-hearted camp, marched right past those who were weeping at the door of the tabernacle, and went into his tent to have sex. A prophet of God took his spear and ran right through Zimri and his lady friend.

And people say they don't read the Bible because it's boring!

Today the liberated church says God was more severe on our forefathers, but now He has only grace to bestow on us. I do thank God for His grace, or we might all be destroyed.

But God is not some big ogre in the sky who will take a smack in the face anytime we want to give Him one. God's character is truth and justice, and He does not change with the circumstances. "For the Lord is good; his mercy is everlasting; and his truth endureth to all generations" (Psalm 100:5).

To those in rebellion within the church who feel God will forgive them because they are really only trying to find a better way, remember these stories.

In The Eye Of The Storm

Some people reading this book have experienced great spiritual victory over pride and are patting themselves on the back. Take heed, tomorrow you may walk out the door and fall flat on your face again by falling into temptation.

Spiritual victory is like being in the eye of a hurricane. When I was a child, we lived in Florida. I remember what it was like to be in the eye of the hurricane. The wind and rain were incredible. Trees fell over the front of our house, and I saw trailers and cars flip over. Then, all of a sudden, blue skies, calm winds, and sunshine came from nowhere. But within fifteen or twenty minutes, that old hurricane was back again.

Listen carefully to this. People sometimes get killed because they are deceived about the eye of a hurricane. Thinking the storm is over, they leave their shelter, get trapped in the oncoming storm, and are killed.

Spiritual victory is sometimes like the eye of the hurricane. You can't bask in your victory forever because the storm is still raging.

The Battle For Souls

I've watched people in churches get caught up in spiritual rebellion toward leadership. They go home after church each Sunday and have "roast pastor and deacons" for lunch. While they attack their pastors around the lunch table, their young children sit with them taking it all in.

As the years pass and those children grow into their teen and young adult years, what happens? So often, those children turn their backs on God because mom and dad soured them on spiritual things years before.

Parents, let me remind you that anytime you get caught up in attacking spiritual leadership, there is a battle going on. That battle is not really over whether or not you'll get a new pastor. It's not really a battle over whether or not your side will win. It's a battle over the souls of your children who daily observe your attitudes and spirit.

When the devil can get Christians to rebel against spiritual leadership, it's just a matter of time before he will lay hold of their offspring.

I admonish you today to put away your spiritual pride and get out where the battle is. Stay in the fight. The battles won't be over until Jesus returns in the clouds of glory.

Remember, the battle is never for buildings, money, or position: The battle is always for souls.

PART II

The Challenge

INTRODUCTION

In the first half of this book I discussed the problem of carnality that is so prevalent in the body of Christ today.

It's not my intention to labor you down with negatives. But I've always believed that we must first diagnose the problem before the cure can be prescribed.

Paul was the chief New Testament writer to the Church of Jesus Christ. Paul loved the Church so much that he said he would gladly spend and be spent for them. Through Paul's writings we see the character of God displayed to His children.

What kind of Church does Christ want? Paul says when speaking of Christ, "That he might present it to himself a glorious church, not having spot, or wrinkle, or any such thing; but that it should be holy and without blemish" (Ephesians 5:27). That is the Church for which Christ is returning. Does it sound like the church you attend?

Paul feared, "Lest when I come, I shall not find you such as I would, and that I shall be found unto you such as ye would not; lest there be debates, envyings, wraths, strifes, backbitings, whisperings, swellings, tumults: and lest, when I come again, my God will humble me among you, and that I shall bewail many which have sinned already, and have not repented of the uncleanness and fornication and lasciviousness which they have committed'' (2 Corinthians 12:20-21).

Paul reminded the Church that if they preached any other gospel they would be cursed. He told them to examine themselves and to have no fellowship with those who ''walked disorderly.'' He encouraged them to live in holiness.

In light of Paul's teaching, I would like to present a challenge to every believer. The first half of this book has dealt with words and ideas that don't go together. Let's consider in the next six chapters some powerful words that *do* go together.

Chapter 7

COMPLETE CONFESSION

When I was ten years old, I had an accident while riding my ten-speed bike down a steep gravel-covered hill. My friends and I were riding about thirty miles an hour, laughing and having a big time. One of them shouted something at me, and I turned around to answer him. WHAM! I hit the back of a parked car and flew over the top of it landing on my face. I was one bloody, dirty, scraped-up, wiped-out little kid.

My mother thought I had broken my nose so she took me to the hospital. Nothing was broken; but, boy, did that doctor do a scrubbing on me! He said he was afraid of infection setting in because of all that dirt in my wounds. He scrubbed my face, arms, and chest with a brush until I cried.

"Doc, what are you doing?" I protested.

"I'm getting the dirt out," he said. "Once it's all out, you'll heal without scarring or infection." Never have I been scrubbed like that!

Sure enough, within two weeks, all those massive scabs were gone. No scarring. No infection. Incredible!

Confession is like a good scrubbing.

Complete confession is God's way of cleaning out the dirt. Although it hurts, it only lasts for a little while.

God's Word says, "If we confess our sins, he is faithful and just to forgive us our sins, and to cleanse us from all unrighteousness" (1 John 1:9).

A Partial Confession

One of the problems among many Christians today is that they want to give *half confessions*. Let's look at the difference between a half confession and a complete confession.

Ananias and Sapphira were a husband and wife team. They sold a possession for a certain price but kept back part of the price for themselves. When Ananias brought the money to the apostles, he laid it at their feet as though it were the total amount.

Then Peter said, "Ananias, Satan has filled your heart. When you claimed this was the full price, you were lying to the Holy Spirit. The property was yours to sell or not, as you wished. And after selling it, it was yours to decide how much to give. How could you do a thing like this? You weren't lying to us, but to God" (Acts 5:3-4 *TLB*).

The Bible says when Ananias heard this he fell down and died.

I have a feeling that God wasn't upset because Ananias and Sapphira had only given *part* of their money. Some believers in the early church were probably like many Christians today—they didn't give *any* of their money away. I think God was upset because of their half truth—their half confession. Later on in that passage, Sapphira also told half a story; and she, too, fell dead at Peter's feet.

Proverbs 28:13 says, "He that covereth his sins shall not prosper: but whoso confesseth and forsaketh them shall have mercy."

God said, "Woe to the rebellious children, saith the Lord, that take counsel, but not of me; and that cover with a covering, but not of my spirit, that they may add sin to sin" (Isaiah 30:1). As long as someone hides sin, he cannot be clothed in the righteousness of God. In other words, you can't paint over rust. No matter how many layers of paint you use, eventually the rust will wear through.

David said in Psalm 66:18, "If I regard iniquity in my heart, the Lord will not hear me." Sooner or later hidden sin will rot through and desecrate the precious things of the Lord. The person who hides his sin is only adding sin to sin, layer upon layer.

For instance, the person who tells a lie must continue to lie in order to cover up the original untruth. Sin is a root that only bears rotten fruit. One sin leads to another.

A Mask Of Sin

Have you ever heard anyone use this remark, "I'm so confused that I just don't know what to do"? Despairing confusion is often a mask for hidden sin. "We lie down in our shame, and our confusion covereth us: for we have sinned against the Lord our God" (Jeremiah 3:25).

God showed me once, through a young lady my wife and I had been counseling, that despairing confusion is often a mask for hidden sin. This gal looked and acted like a real spiritual person. But inwardly, this young lady harbored the sin of immorality in her heart. Time after time she came to us, and we counseled and prayed with her. But after uncovering layer after layer of problems, we always got down to the root—this immorality thing. Then she would throw up her hands and say, "Oh, I'm so confused. I just don't know what to do."

Every time she pulled that little "confusion trick" out of her bag, my wife and I would look at each other and say, "Well, that's it for another day." As long as she was unwilling to drop the mask of confusion and deal with her root problem of immorality, we could not help her.

Another time a young man came up to me after one of my meetings at a Bible College.

"Mr. Wilkerson," he said, "I really need to talk to you."

So the two of us went into a side room and sat down. Before I could even ask his name, he buried his head in his hands and said, "I'm so confused about God's will for my life. I really don't know what to do."

Right away the verse from Jeremiah 3:25 registered in my mind. "We lie down in our shame, and our confusion covereth us; for we have sinned against the Lord our God."

I looked at him for a minute and then said, "Okay, here's your problem. You are masking hidden sin in your life. If you'll get rid of that sin, the confusion will go away and God will tell you what to do."

Oh, man, he got so upset!

"What do you mean?" he questioned me. "I'm a Bible college student. I'm ready to graduate and go into the ministry. I can't believe you would say that to me."

"Are you confused?" I asked.

"Yes," he said.

"Are you at a place of despair because of your confusion?"

"Yes, I am," he said.

"Well, I'm only telling you what the Bible says." And I gave it to him again.... "Now," I said, "if you want to be honest with me, we can continue. But if you don't, we're both wasting our time because I don't know any other way to get you out of this. So, do you want to quit now or go on?"

"Well," he said, "maybe I do have a few problems here and there."

"Okay, what are they?" I asked.

"Well," he said, "I guess I don't have any more than the next guy does. But I have struggled at times with lust."

"Are you married?"

"Yes, I am," he said.

"You mean God has given you a wife, and you're still lusting after other women?"

"Well, yes, from time to time," he continued.

"Okay, what has this lust driven you to do?"

"Well," he said, "I've got to be honest. I've struggled a little bit with pornography."

"You're a Bible student, ready to graduate and go into full-time ministry, and you're struggling with pornography? When was the last time that you read dirty literature—years ago?"

"No, a little more often than that."

"Every week?"

"Yeah."

"Every day?"

"Yeah. I guess I'm really into that stuff."

"Well, what else has reading this pornography led you into?" I asked.

"I'm ashamed to tell you this. I also go to the bath houses here in the community."

"THE BATH HOUSES—YOU GO TO THE BATH HOUSES?" I said wide-eyed. "What else?"

"Well, sometimes I beat my wife," he said.

By the time we were through, we had peeled through layers of lusts of the flesh—pornography, bath houses, and wife abuse. He got to the root of the problem, confessed it all, and got rid of it. Today, God is using that young couple in the ministry, but it never could have happened if complete confession had not taken place.

Hidden No Longer

Let's look now at what I call a *forced* confession. In the Old Testament, there is a story about a man named Achan who was forced to make a confession for his hidden sin. Achan disobeyed God by stealing "a goodly Babylonish garment, and two hundred shekels of silver, and a wedge of gold of fifty shekels weight" (Joshua 7:21). The Bible says he hid it in his tent.

God had commanded Israel not to remove anything from the destroyed city of Jericho because everything in it was cursed. But Achan thought he could secretly get away with his theft. However, because of his hidden sin, "the anger of the Lord was kindled against the children of Israel" (Joshua 7:1).

In sackcloth and ashes, Joshua, Israel's leader, pleaded with God to tell him why Israel experienced defeat in her battle with Ai and why He was angry with them. And God answered, "Israel hath sinned, and they have also transgressed my covenant which I commanded them: for they have even taken of the accursed thing, and have also stolen, and dissembled also, and they have put it even among their own stuff" (Joshua 7:11).

The next morning, Joshua called each tribe, then each family, then each man to give account of himself. It's incredible to see how God proceeded to weed out the culprit. Achan must have been shaking in his boots as the questioning narrowed from three million Jews down to about fifty. "Be sure your sin will find you out" (Numbers 32:23).

Finally, Achan and his family stood before Joshua. "And Joshua said unto Achan, My son, give, I pray thee, glory to the Lord God of Israel, and make confession unto him; and tell me now what thou hast done; hide it not from me" (Joshua 7:19).

Confronted with his sin, Achan answered Joshua, "Indeed I have sinned against the Lord of Israel" (Joshua 7:20).

This is what I mean by a *forced confession*.

God's Word tells us that one day *every* knee shall bow and *every* tongue confess that Jesus Christ is Lord. (See Philippians 2:10-11.) That day will be one of forced confessions. But God is not looking for robots. He does not want to force anyone to do anything against his will. The only reason God backed Achan into a corner was to keep his sin from affecting all of Israel.

It's hard to believe, isn't it, that one man's sin could affect a nation? What's even harder to believe is that Achan was willing to allow the entire nation to be jeopardized because of that sin.

In verse twenty-five of that same passage, Joshua asked Achan, "Why hast thou troubled us?" Hidden sin always troubles someone. It not only troubles the sinful individual with day-in and day-out guilt, but it troubles everyone around that person. It messes up the whole family.

What Achan thought was well hidden turned out to be exposed to the nation; and, as a result, cost him his life.

Confession Means Restitution

One night at the end of a crusade meeting, I gave the altar call. I asked those who wanted to accept Christ as their Savior to come to the altar for prayer.

While others were on their way down, one man in the back of the auditorium practically crawled over people to get out in the aisle. I thought he was coming to the altar; but, instead, he turned and ran out the back door. About thirty minutes later, I was still at the altar praying with people when I looked up and saw this same man running down the aisle. He came over to me and asked for prayer. So we prayed, and he accepted Christ into his life. But I was curious about where he had gone.

"Why did you leave and then come back?" I asked him.

"Well," he said, "I work for the Safeway market about a mile from here. For about a year, I've been skimming a little off the top. The owner has had complete confidence in me and has never really noticed how much money I've stolen. But tonight I wanted to become a Christian and get my heart right with God. I just couldn't ask God to forgive me until I made things right with my boss.

"So I ran out to my car, drove down to the store, and told my boss I had to talk to him. I told him what I had done, that I had been to a church meeting that night, and that I wanted to make it right with him and God. I told him I would work for forty hours a week for the next eight weeks without a paycheck so that I could pay him back.

"My boss was so shocked that he began to cry, and then he forgave me for my whole debt. But I didn't leave until he promised he would let me work for those next two months without pay.

"I can't tell you how happy I am that this load is lifted off my back and God has forgiven me. I'm not guilty anymore!"

Confession for that man meant restitution.

Now I'm not saying that a person *must* make restitution *before* he asks God to forgive him. Restitution is difficult in our own flesh. But once we have received God's forgiveness and His grace, restitution becomes a natural thing to do.

In fact, once we have accepted Christ into our life, we are commanded to "go and tell" others that they too may come to the saving knowledge of Jesus Christ for themselves. It's hard to witness to someone whom you have robbed, ripped off, or defrauded in any way.

The Power Of Confession

One of the things that amazed me most about the man who first made restitution was the change in his countenance. When he left the church, his facial expression was tense—almost horrified. But when he returned, he was smiling and relaxed. Joy and relief beamed from his face because all the pain, hurt, and guilt had vanished. His face reflected the change in his heart and life.

That's what I was talking about earlier. Confession cleanses. It cleanses the mind and the emotions, along with producing great spiritual power.

Maybe you have recently come to the Lord—yet there's a nagging hurt from your past. Possibly you have struggled with confusion. Once again, let me point you to 1 John 1:9, "If we confess our sins He is faithful and just to forgive us our sin and cleanse us from all unrighteousness.''

I believe God is saying to all of us that if we will confess every sin that we can remember commiting, He will forgive us for those sins and even for the sins we have forgotten about.

God is willing to completely cleanse us if we are ready to give Him a complete confession.

Chapter 8

RADICAL REPENTANCE

The only effective way out of a carnal lifestyle is God's way. King David said to God, "Wash me throughly from mine iniquity, and cleanse me from my sin.... Create in me a clean heart, O God; and renew a right spirit within me" (Psalm 51:2,10).

In the last chapter, we learned that confession is the first step out of the world and into God's presence. Following our confession of sin, we must now be willing to *repent* of our sin.

A young man once came to me after one of my meetings and said, "Mr. Wilkerson, God really changed my life tonight. I made a 150-degree turn-around for the Lord." I chuckled and thought to myself that he'd be just a bit off on the day of judgment. God is not looking for a 150 or a 155-degree turn. He's looking for a complete 180-degree turnaround—a complete change of heart, mind, and lifestyle.

A repentant person is one who is sorry he has sinned—so sorry that he's ready to change. The problem is, too often, we mistake confession for repentance. Repentance goes beyond confession. A repentant person willingly accepts the radical change—no matter what the consequence or loss of prestige.

An Act Of Repentance

I received a copy of the following letter from a fifty-five-year-old man who was estranged from his wife and family. Under conviction from the Holy Spirit to confess his sin and repent of his past, he wrote:

> To each member of my family,
>
> Since Christmas I have had many hours to think of my sins and weaknesses which have brought us to this sad time in our lives. I have allowed conditions to continue that I should have stopped years ago.
>
> I have not been the prize husband or father. In fact, all you can really say about me is that I have paid the bills.
>
> What I am about to ask won't be easy, but with God's help it is possible. I have recently learned that the authority God has given me as husband and father carries grave responsibilities. I have learned it is my responsibility to find a solution to the problems my family now faces.

You have said I was an ignorant man. You were right. You have said I was a liar. Again you were right. I am ashamed of these things. But I don't have to stay that way.

The following request will be the hard part for you. In shame, I ask to be forgiven for the torment I have caused—for my insensitive attitude toward my wife, for the ignorance of the responsibility of authority and love God wanted me to show. Forgive me for my wagging tongue which I used to make myself look better. Forgive me for neglecting the responsibility of handling the family finances and making unwise investments.

What I will do, with God's help, is:

I will not lie anymore.

I will be strong in the Lord and do His will.

I will refuse to participate in gossip.

I will take the burden of financial responsibility.

I will instruct members of my family who cannot forgive me to give their anger to God and let Him deal with it.

I know that God has forgiven me, and with His help we can become the family He wants us to be. I love each one of you.

This letter typifies a man who has experienced radical repentance. Nothing is more joyous than knowing that God has forgiven us of our sins and, by His grace, will restore us to wholeness.

Why Radical Repentance?

Sin breaks God's heart. In the first book of the Bible, the Spirit of God allows us to come into the secret place of God's thoughts. "And God saw that the wickedness of man was great in the earth, and that every imagination of the thoughts of his heart was only evil continually ... and it grieved him at his heart" (Genesis 6:5-6). God's heart was filled with pain, and He was sorry He had made man.

Again in Ezekiel 6:9, we read how God grieves over our sin: "I am broken with their whorish heart, which hath departed from me."

Paul said, "Godly sorrow worketh repentance to salvation ... but the sorrow of the world worketh death" (2 Corinthians 7:10). Godly sorrow comes to us because we have caught a glimpse of the pain God experiences over our sin. Sorrow that causes us to change brings salvation. Worldly sorrow (being sorry because our sin has been exposed), without radical change, is worthless. Only godly repentance will restore us to a right relationship with God.

Another reason we must experience radical repentance is that it will restore us to a right relationship with ourselves and others.

Listen to what one man who struggled with defeat wrote:

Mr. Wilkerson, I needed to hear the messages you delivered recently about repentance. For the last week, I have been under conviction to make things right with God and others. It hasn't been easy, but as you said, surgery always hurts.

I'm tired of playing games. It's too hard for me to sin on Saturday night and act like a Christian on Sunday morning. The games are taking a toll on me spiritually.

In the last few days, I have written letters of apology, asked forgiveness from people I have wronged, and even sent money to people I have stolen from.

Until now I have been unable to get victory over drinking and sexual immorality. I want to gain freedom from these sins, and I want to be accountable. All this has been really hard for me, but I know it was necessary to get my life in order again. I also know that nothing is impossible with God.

I know the man who wrote this letter, and I know that, for him, confession of sin was not enough. This man had to willfully turn from his phony lifestyle to follow hard after Christ. It cost him dearly. But today he is a new man in Christ.

You, too, can make the break from a sinful lifestyle. It will cost you dearly, too. But the life that follows will be more rewarding than any way of life you have ever known before. "If we walk in the light, as he is in the light, we have fellowship one with another, and the blood of Jesus Christ his Son cleanseth us from all sin" (1 John 1:7).

Praise God! This means continual grace will be directed toward you who walk in God's light.

The Secret Of Staying Free

One of the most powerful benefits of repentance is that we can take our eyes off our problems and begin to focus on the new life. Many testimonies spend more time focusing on things of the past—drugs, sexual sin, etc.—than they do on the joy of the new life in Christ.

In John 20:11, we read, "Mary stood without at the sepulchre weeping: and as she wept, she stooped down, and looked into the sepulchre." Mary had her eyes on the hurt, on the pain, on the tomb where Jesus had lain. Even though the body was gone, Mary still had her eyes focused on death.

Unfortunately, many of us are like Mary. We live without hope. Even though sin (death) has been confessed and is now in the past, we live with the past clearly in focus.

Mary could not see the risen Christ until she turned her eyes away from the sepulchre. Neither can we.

When I was teaching my little boy how to ride his bike, I told him, "Son, keep your eyes on that mail box down the street and ride toward it." As long as he kept his eyes on his goal, he could balance that bike without the training wheels. But as soon as he looked back to see if I was still holding on, he and that old bike would fall over. Then I would repeat the instruction. "No, no, keep your eyes in front of you. Keep your eyes on your goal."

The apostle Paul told us the same thing. "Forgetting those things which are behind, and reaching forth unto those things which are before.... I press toward the mark for the prize of the high calling of God in Christ Jesus" (Philippians 3:13-14).

Our goal is to press on to victory—victory over sin, self, and shame.

Heavenly Treasures Vs. Earthly Riches

As I close this chapter, I want to tell you what confession and repentance cost a dear friend of mine. This man is a very, very wealthy person. Several years ago, he had a marvelous conversion. As a result of his new life in Christ, this man turned away from his sinful past.

After walking with the Lord for several years, he became concerned about some jade, gold, and ivory sculptures he had previously purchased on his travels around the world. Several of these pieces were replicas of ancient gods, goddesses, and idols of heathen lands. He knew these were not pleasing to God.

As the spiritual leader in his home, this man did not feel the presence of these sculptures was a good influence to his children or to those who visited their family. He decided to destroy over one million dollars worth of costly art. He broke them, crushed them into powder, burned some, and threw others away.

When he had finished, he told me he felt a new release in his life and a new freedom in his home. Christ reigned supreme in that home.

Some people said, "A million dollars! Why didn't he just sell them?" Let me ask you a question. Would you sell something to someone knowing it would hurt him also? That was his point.

It cost this man over a million dollars to repent, but he was willing to pay the price.

I wonder what price each of us would be willing to pay to purify, cleanse, and turn away the evil things from a past life.

David said, "Who shall ascend into the hill of the Lord? or who shall stand in his holy place? He that hath clean hands; and a pure heart.... He shall receive the blessing from the Lord, and righteousness from the God of his salvation" (Psalm 24:3-5).

In the light of all eternity, is what you are holding onto worth keeping you from blessing, righteousness, and your own salvation?

An Unbroken Promise

God uses ex-sinners. This is the power and the promise of repentance. Jesus said, "Behold, I stand at the door, and knock: if any man hear my voice, and open the door, I will come in to him, and will sup with him, and he with me" (Revelation 3:20).

God promises this to *any man* who will come.

Some of us may question who is the worst sinner among us. The apostle Paul admitted being the chief of all sinners. "This is a faithful saying, and worthy of all acceptation, that Christ Jesus came into the world to save sinners; of whom I am chief" (1 Timothy 1:15).

God can use anyone, but Christ must first be allowed into a person's heart. Some will say, "But I've done so many wrong things." So did the apostle Paul. So did Rich Wilkerson. But Jesus Christ can change all that.

"If any man be in Christ, he is a *new creature:* old things are passed away; behold, *all things* are become new" (2 Corinthians 5:17, italics mine).

God promises us a new shot at life—another brand-new opportunity.

To those who have been living a half-in-half-out, "carnal Christian" lifestyle: *If you will come to a place of radical repentance,* God will do in your life what you cannot do for yourself.

Those who are unwilling to repent are known as "enemies of the cross of Christ: whose end is destruction" (Philippians 3:18-19).

The decision and the promises are yours. I pray that in reading this chapter, the Spirit of God has convinced you to make the right choice.

Chapter 9

PRAYING PEOPLE

If I were to ask a "carnal Christian" how his prayer life is, he would probably answer, "What prayer life?"

The reason he has no prayer life is that prayer produces holiness, and holiness and worldliness cannot coexist. Prayer produces clean living. It bears fruit for the kingdom and is pleasing to God. Prayer links a man's heart to the heart of God.

Paul tells us that one day, "Every knee should bow ... and every tongue should confess that Jesus Christ is Lord" (Philippians 2:10-11). *Every knee and every tongue* means just that. However, that action will be one that is enforced. Until that day comes, those of us who call ourselves Christians must seek to commune with God in humility and earnestness as King David did.

In Psalm 42, David lets us overhear his prayer to God. "As the hart panteth after the water brooks, so panteth my soul after thee, O God. My soul thirsteth for God, for the living God: when shall I come and appear before God?" (verses 1-2). "Oh, God," David is saying, "it's You and You alone I desire."

113

Since God is holy, time spent with Him produces holiness in a person's life and results in hatred for sin. When a person hates what God hates, it is impossible for him to be a carnal Christian.

Full And Overflowing

Prayer also produces a heart full of *joy.* Who among us would not want a heart full of joy? In R. A. Torrey's book, *How To Pray,* he says, "Prayer in the name of Jesus Christ is the way He Himself has appointed for His disciples to obtain fullness of joy." Picture someone you know who is joyful. Coming into their presence is like contacting an electrical machine charged with gladness.

Torrey continues, "Why is it that prayer in the name of Christ brings such fullness of joy? In part, because we get what we ask. But that is not the only reason, nor is it the greatest. It makes God real. When we ask something definite of God, and He gives it, how real God becomes! He is right there! It is blessed to have a God who is real and not merely an idea."[1]

Those who know me know I am a happy person. I love to have a good time. But I always struggle with people who are super pious. Maybe it's because I feel they are only trying to appear holy. People cannot be fooled by the *appearance* of holiness. Certainly God isn't fooled. Holiness is not a quality a person can fake.

An Ever-Widening Supply Of Love

Something else happens in a person's life when he cultivates his prayer life. He develops a real love for souls. From a kneeling position selfish desires take on a different perspective. For instance, if I were to go to God in prayer and say, "I want a boat, oh God, I really want a boat." Soon I start thinking about water skis to go with the boat. But the longer I stay on my knees, the more God changes my heart. God reminds me of the starving children in North Africa and the large population there that has never heard the Gospel.

Before long, my selfishness falls away, and my desires line up with God's. Now I pray what is on God's heart. "Oh, God, forget the boat. Give me instead the power to win a soul to You today."

When I was growing up, my parents and I lived in the Bahamas where they were serving as missionaries. A tall, burly Texan named Talmadge Butler stayed in our home once a week. He was a pilot for the missionaries on the islands, and our island was centrally located. Many nights Mom, Dad, and Talmadge would stay up late talking, laughing, and then praying. I used to stand at my bedroom door and listen. Once they started to pray, they prayed and prayed and prayed.

Finally, Talmadge would make his way up to my room where there were twin beds. I would fake sleeping and watch in the dim light as this hulk of a man slipped down to his knees beside the bed. Very quietly he continued in prayer, "Dear God, please give me these islands for Christ. I want to see the people saved and changed." Then he'd begin to pray for Africa. He had a burning desire to go to Africa and knew all the places in West Africa by name. I remember him calling them out to God—Liberia, Togo, Senegal…. Then he would weep and weep and weep.

When he stopped weeping, he began to pray for me. "Dear God, make Rich into a man of God. May he see many souls saved." Often Talmadge Butler would fall asleep on his knees.

Years later, Talmadge got his desire. He and his family served God in Africa for years. Many, many young people were called into full-time service under Talmadge's ministry.

One night back in Kenosha, Wisconsin, our family was at a restaurant when my father was called to the telephone. Dad was gone for a long time. Slipping out into the lobby, I saw Dad standing there with his head in his hands and tears streaming down his face. He had learned that the plane carrying Talmadge and his family back to the States had gone down in the ocean and only pieces of it were found.

That night when I got back to my room, I knelt beside my bed and thanked God for this man's influence on my life. He was a man full of joy and full of love for others.

Living Examples

Our church in Tacoma, Washington, is pastored by Dr. Fulton Buntain. Last year, Dr. Buntain became impressed with the need for more prayer in his own personal life and ministry (his church numbers over 5,000). God spoke to him and asked for a thousand people to pray with him for one hour a day. I can testify to the new vibrancy and anointing that is happening now in the worship services.

Dr. David Maines, of the television program *100 Huntley Street* in Canada, promised God years ago that he would spend one hour in prayer for every hour that he appeared on television. Every day, Dr. Maines goes to his office around 5:00 a.m. and spends that time in prayer. Then he spends nearly an hour a day in prayer with his guests before they go on nationwide television. His ministry is having a profound impact on others because of his dedication to prayer. During my many crusades in Canada, I always meet people who have accepted Jesus Christ as a result of Dr. Maines' television ministry.

Dick Eastman, author of the book, *No Easy Road,* has a worldwide ministry called *Change The World School Of Prayer.* Dick has been used by God to motivate multitudes of people to pray. When I was a twelve-year-old boy, Dick and his wife Delores, who is my cousin, came from North Central Bible College to be my father's youth pastors. Dick was twenty years old then. Because of his influence on those kids, many learned the power of prayer and were changed by God's touch.

One summer while my parents were on vacation, I stayed with Dick and Dee. They had a little, fifteen-year-old, wiped-out trailer home. It was so small they could hardly turn around in it. I mean it was small! Dick was finishing his schooling at the university and holding down a full-time job as the youth minister. One morning around 3:00 a.m., I got up to go to the bathroom. The door was partially opened and a light was on. I pushed the door a little to see why the light was on. There was Dick using the only private place in the trailer as his prayer closet. Each night that week, at 3:00 a.m., Dick prayed on his knees in his "prayer closet."

Another person who has been an example to me all my life is my godly father. I've seen him in many situations, but I've never seen this man's character change. He loves God and believes in the power of prayer. I remember as a child seeing pastors from the community—both protestant and Catholic backgrounds—filter into my father's office for prayer. Many of them came on the sly because their congregations would never approve of their association. But Dad never betrayed their confidence. They came to pray—and pray they did. Sometimes all afternoon and into the night I would hear them praying and crying out to God.

After I was grown and gone from home, my wife Robyn and I were invited to a surprise twenty-fifth wedding anniversary for my parents. When we got to the house, we tip-toed up to the front door. To the left of the door was my Dad's office. As I put my hand on the doorknob, I peeked in his office window. I could see him through the sheer curtains. He was on his knees, and I could hear him crying out to God for his family. Right there on that doorstep, I bowed my head and thanked God for all the hundreds of times I had heard my father pray for us.

Seeking God takes time. But there are no short-cuts. Each of us needs to find individual direction from God.

Finding Direction Through Prayer

God wants to communicate with us. "Call unto me, and I will answer thee, and shew thee great and mighty things, which thou knowest not" (Jeremiah 33:3). It is not within the father-heart of God to keep His will for our lives a secret. "Call … and I will answer."

In my own prayer life, I have found some effective steps toward hearing from God.

First, I must come into God's presence with a clean heart. David said, "If I regard iniquity in my heart, the Lord will not hear me" (Psalm 67:6). I want God to hear me. I assume you do, too. Therefore, we must pray as David did, "Wash me throughly from mine iniquity, and cleanse me from my sin" (Psalm 51:2).

Secondly, I let the devil know that he is not welcome in this conversation I'm having with God. So I resist him vehemently. James 4:7 tells us to "submit yourselves therefore to God. Resist the devil, and he will flee from you."

I resist the devil with the Word of God just like Jesus did in the wilderness. (Read Matthew 4:1-11.) The following verses should be memorized to silence Satanic voices when in prayer: Isaiah 54:17; 59:19;

Romans 5:20; 2 Corinthians 10:3-5; 1 John 4:4.

Next we must die to our own fleshly desires and reasonings. God alone knows what we need. "Man looketh on the outward appearance, but the Lord looketh on the heart" (1 Samuel 16:7).

Many times I have prayed for a specific need with a predisposed idea of how God should answer my prayer. When I'm aware of what I'm doing, I stop praying in that direction. I know that my firmly established desires sometimes do not line up with God's will for my life.

God does not want us to come to Him for His signature of approval on all of our selfish desires. He longs to discuss His will with us.

"Put me in remembrance: let us plead together" (Isaiah 43:26a).

Now I am ready to communicate with God. Hebrews 4:16 says that I may "come boldly unto the throne of grace ... and find ... help in time of need."

Communicating with God is the highlight of my day. To come into the presence of the living God and find a "friendly audience" is awe-inspiring.

I find that God always has direction for me. He always wants to be included in my plans and decisions. He always has time for my insignificant request.

Lastly, I must act upon the word God has given me. In Mark 16:15, Jesus said to His disciples, "Go ye into all the world, and preach the gospel to every creature." Verse 20 tells how they responded. "And they went forth, and preached every where." Miracles took place when the disciples obeyed God. I believe we will see answers to prayer and signs and wonders when we, too, obey God.

A Word To Pastors

Moses was a great man of God and a leader of many people. He had one problem, however, that many of us preachers have. Moses depended on his gifts rather than on God.

Jerry Rose, the director of Channel 38 Christian television in Chicago, shared this insight with me. In Numbers 20, God's people were complaining, thirsty, and wanting to go back to Egypt. God told Moses, "Take the rod, and gather thou the assembly together, thou, and Aaron thy brother, and speak ye unto the rock before their eyes; and it shall give forth his water, and thou shalt bring forth to them water out of the rock; so thou shalt give the congregation and their beasts drink" (verse 8).

Instead, Moses smote the rock. The rod he used to hit the rock was a gift to him from God. He knew what would happen if he used the rod. But if Moses had *spoken* to the rock, he would have had to depend entirely on God.

Moses and his people were upset, so he wanted to go with the "sure" thing. In spite of Moses' action, God was faithful and supplied their need; but it cost Moses the joy of seeing the promised land.

Human reasoning never produces powerful ministries. The church can spot a phony in the pulpit. E. M. Bounds says in *Power Through Prayer,* ''The preacher must primarily be a man of prayer. In the school of prayer, only the heart can learn to preach. No learning can make up for the failure to pray. No earnestness, no diligence, no study, no gifts will supply its lack.

''Talking to men for God is a great thing, but talking to God for men is still greater. He who has not learned well how to talk to God for men will never talk well—with real success—to men for God. More than this, prayerless words, both in and out of the pulpit are deadening.''[2]

The Purpose Of Prayer In Preaching

Recently, I talked to Dr. David Larson, professor of pastoral theology and preaching at Trinity Evangelical Seminary in Deerfield, Illinois. He is a tremendous man of God and has pastored some of the largest churches in America. I said, ''Dr. Larson, what is lacking in our pulpits today?''

Without hesitation, Dr. Larson answered, ''Rich, we are lacking simple, purposeful preaching.''

Prayer brings purpose into preaching. A clear purpose existed in the messages Jesus preached. After many hours in prayer, Jesus knew what message God wanted delivered to His people. ''That they might know thee the only true God, and Jesus Christ, whom thou hast sent'' (John 17:3).

John Hyde was a mighty preacher. He *prayed* persuasive preaching into existence. He would pray and preach and pray some more. People called him Praying Hyde. Weakened by foodless days and sleepless nights, Praying Hyde pleaded with God to "give me souls or I die."

Today, hundreds of Christians are walking out of their churches on Sunday morning saying, "Boy, wasn't that a heavy message? What did he say?"

Another shakes his head and replies, "I don't know, but it must have been spiritual because no one could understand it."

Carnality results because Christians do not obey God's Word. But how can someone obey what he does not know? What a shame that some spend one hour a week in a worship service and come away without finding purposeful direction for living.

It will take more than one hour a week in church to walk free from carnality. We must be "praying people" who demand better leaders because we live better lives for God.

Recently while preaching at a minister's convention in Texas, I watched the Holy Spirit stir over 1500 people to tears. God had given me a message to deliver on the need for prayer in our churches.

The conviction of the Holy Spirit flooded that auditorium. As I gave the call at the end of the service for ministers to get back to the basics of prayer in their own lives, hundreds stepped into the aisles weeping before God. I could hear them praying— "God, I want You in my life ... I want You to work in our church ... I want a spirit of prayer to fall on our congregation ... Let it begin in me.''

We can't point a finger at our brothers or sisters and hope they will feel the need to pray. It must begin individually in each of our hearts.

Am I a prayer warrior?

Carnal Christianity ends when prayer begins!

Chapter 10

FAITHFUL FOLLOWERS

Marie Johnsrud is a tremendous follower of God. Marie was a missionary to Upper Volta, West Africa for thirty-four years. While in Upper Volta, Marie worked as a midwife, nurse, English teacher, print shop manager, worship service leader, and music instructor. She rode a three-wheeled motorbike into primitive areas to teach simple hygiene. During Africa's famine years, Marie hauled grain all over Upper Volta in a pick-up truck. At times she would deliver coffins for funerals or transport the sick to hospitals.

In a mud hut, without electricity or modern facilities, Marie translated English material into the Mouri language. She also typed all the manuscripts for the complete Mouri Bible—twice. One church gave Marie an electric typewriter, and she graciously received it. But since there was no electricity where she lived, she sold it to buy things for the needy.

Several years ago, Marie felt the Lord was telling her to return home. Feeling somewhat guilty for leaving her work, she prayed most of the night inquiring of the Lord for clear direction. The next morning while reading Scripture, she opened to Jeremiah 4, and her eyes fell on verse 6: "Retire, stay not." Marie received those words as from the Lord and returned to Tacoma, Washington.

My in-laws went to the airport to pick her up. Marie, now in her middle sixties, got off the plane with a giant smile on her face and a brown paper sack filled with all her worldly goods.

Since this faithful follower has been home, she has taken up the work of the Lord here also. On holidays, Marie prepares food for the poor through St. Leo's Church in Tacoma, Washington. She plays the accordian and visits inmates at the Pierce County jail every week. Each week she teaches Asian immigrants to read and write for the Tacoma Literacy Council. She entertains at convalescent homes as a member of a local bell choir. She reads books and other publications to seven ladies who are unable to see. Through a weekly program, she instructs elementary-age girls to be good citizens with good character. She helps with the weekly newsletter at the church and volunteers at a charitable organization that supports a feeding program for deprived children overseas.

Each week, Marie spends time with our children. She takes them on the bus to town, and they stop at the dime store. Our kids look forward to their weekly outing with Auntie Marie.

When Marie retired, my wife and I contributed $150 a month support to her, but we did it through the local church so she wouldn't find out where the money came from. We knew she would never take money from us. One day, I was visiting Aunt Marie at her home. She was busy sending out birthday cards, which she regularly does (by the hundreds) all over the world. I noticed she had her checkbook beside her and was writing out checks.

"Aunt Marie," I said, "what are you doing?"

"Rich," she said, "you'll never believe this. God has provided me with an extra $150 a month. Now I'm able to send ten of my former students, who are now national missionaries in West Africa, $15 each month. For years, people have supported me, and now I'm able to financially support others."

I had to leave and get alone with God. I felt like such a sinner in her presence.

When I speak of "faithful followers," I think about people like Marie Johnsrud, whom the world has never known. It's the Marie Johnsruds of this world who make this Christian gospel go forward.

God is looking for servants who are willing to lay aside their own personal wants and desires and faithfully say, "Lord, not my will but Thine be done." I suppose the day that Marie walks through the "pearly gates," the red carpet will stretch for miles as that "great cloud of witnesses" applauds her entrance.

Taking The First Step

A faithful follower is nothing more than a disciple of Jesus Christ. Before one can live this kind of life, he or she must make that all-important *decision* to become Christ's disciple. Unfortunately, many Christians never really decide. "Therefore, my beloved brethren, be ye stedfast, unmoveable, always abounding in the work of the Lord, forasmuch as ye know that your labour is not in vain in the Lord" (1 Corinthians 15:58).

What Paul meant was make up your mind, and once having done that, don't change it—hang in there!

David said, "O God, my heart is fixed; I will sing and give praise, even with my glory" (Psalm 108:1).

So the first step then is to make a *decision* to go God's way and stick with it.

A Song For The King

The second thing a disciple must do is realize that he is called to *influence* the world.

Earlier in the book, I told you about the prayer life of my friend David Maines, host of *100 Huntley Street* in Toronto, Canada. Years ago, as a young, pioneer pastor of a church in Ontario, David and his little congregation held a Saturday night street meeting. At 5:00 p.m. each Saturday evening, in a town of about five thousand, people gathered to listen to David's message.

One day David saw in the newspaper that the Queen of England was coming to Canada and that her motorcade would pass through their town about the same time their weekly meeting would take place. David got excited.

Early that afternoon, this little group set up their stage on the corner of Main Street just as they had done in past weeks. Some of the town leaders said, "What are you doing? The Queen is coming through! You can't set this thing up here."

David said he was sorry, but he had a permit from the city fathers saying he could. And he did. He set up his little stage with its speaker system, placed their instruments on it, and put up the Canadian flag and the British Flying Jack.

Sure enough at 5:00 p.m., a large crowd began to gather; and off in the distance, the Queen's motorcade could be seen. As her motorcade got closer and closer, David Maines stepped to the microphone and said, "Good afternoon. Welcome to Bethel Church's weekly Saturday night street meeting. We're glad all of you could come, and we want to welcome our very special guest tonight, the Queen of England. Let's all remove our hats and sing 'God Save The Queen.'"

As the crowd began to sing, the Queen drove by, waving, looking up at David, and wondering what was going on. He smiled and waved back.

When the crowd finished singing, David said, "Now, let's sing that great song to the King of Kings and Lord of Lords, 'How Great Thou Art.'" The crowd joined right in and began singing praise to God. When the singing stopped, no one left. David preached and then invited them to the morning worship service at his little church.

He said that when he drove up to the church the next morning, cars were parked everywhere. That little pioneer church had standing room only.

David Mainse knew it was his responsibility to *influence* his world for Christ, and God rewarded him.

Through television, billboards, radio, and magazines, the world has given us enough of its evil influence. God needs people in this day who will stand up and *influence* people for Him.

Living Sacrifices

To be a faithful follower, you will soon discover what *sacrifice* means in the life of a believer. Paul said,"I beseech you therefore, brethren, by the mercies of God, that you present your bodies a living sacrifice, holy, acceptable unto God, which is your reasonable service" (Romans 12:1).

I remember a night in 1972 in Minneapolis when I knelt by my bed and said, "God, I offer myself to you as a 'living sacrifice.' I'll pay any price. I'll do anything and go anywhere. Whatever, God, I want You! If it means life or death, I will sacrifice everything to the call of God on my life."

God's call for me was to serve Him in full-time Christian ministry. But for most Christians it means being a living *sacrifice* at home, office, school, or factory. It means that God has first say in all of our decisions. Eventually, following after God becomes such a joy and privilege that the believer says with the apostle Paul, "But what things were gain to me, those I counted loss for Christ. Yea doubtless, and I count all things but loss for the excellency of the knowledge of Christ Jesus my Lord: for whom I have suffered the loss of all things" (Philippians 3:7-8).

Continually Committed

It's one thing to sacrifice your life on the altar of God's service, but it's another thing to be *continually committed* to keeping that sacrifice on the altar.

I meet many people who call themselves Christian and who at one time sacrificed their lives to God but have since changed their minds.

Paul said, "For Demas hath forsaken me, having loved this present world, and is departed unto Thessalonica; Crescens to Galatia, Titus unto Dalmatia"(2 Timothy 4:10). At one time, Demas was quite committed to Paul. I'm sure if he was committed to Paul as a friend, it was because Paul had influenced Demas for Christ. But Demas changed his mind. He backed off on his sacrifice to God.

Demas took back his sacrifice because he wasn't continually *committed* to staying true to Christ. Paul said, "I die daily" (1 Corinthians 15:31). Being committed as a faithful follower of Christ is a daily battle. Walking away from the carnal life is also a daily battle.

You can build upon yesterday's successes, but those successes won't keep you committed to God today. You must *daily* commit that living sacrifice to God.

Behind Closed Doors

Another thing God is looking for is people with *integrity* who will become faithful followers—people who will be as honest and upright behind closed doors as they are before others.

131

Leonard Ravenhill tells the story of an evangelist who preached in a large city. On Monday morning, after his meeting, he left his motel room and caught a bus to go into town to do some shopping. As he got on the bus, the driver told him his fare would be 50 cents. The evangelist gave the driver one dollar, and the driver returned three quarters to him. When he sat down and looked at the change in his hand, he realized the driver had given him too much change in return.

The evangelist walked up to the front of the bus and said, "Sir, I'm sorry, but you have given me one quarter too much."

The bus driver took the quarter and replied, "Sir, I didn't make a mistake. I was at your meeting last night and heard you preach. I just wanted to see if you practice what you preach."

Job said, "If I have walked with vanity, or if my foot hath hasted to deceit; let me be weighed in an even balance, that God may know mine integrity" (Job 31:5-6).

David said, "Judge me, O Lord; for I have walked in mine integrity: I have trusted also in the Lord; therefore I shall not slide. Examine me, O Lord, and prove me; try my reins and my heart" (Psalm 26:1-2).

What about your *integrity* in your personal devotions? Do you have a consistent devotional life with God?

What about your *integrity* before your family? What does your wife or husband think of your Christianity?

What about your private thought patterns? Would you be happy to publish your thoughts from the past twenty-four hours?

All these things can only be answered by you. No one else knows what goes on behind your closed doors.

Plum Trees Do Not Bear Apples

Faithful followers are called to be *partakers* with Christ. When Christ comes to dwell within us, He becomes our older brother. "Wherefore thou art no more a servant, but a son; and if a son, then an heir of God through Christ" (Galatians 4:7).

Peter said, "But rejoice, inasmuch as ye are *partakers* of Christ's sufferings; that, when his glory shall be revealed, ye may be glad also with exceeding joy. If you are reproached for the name of Christ, happy are ye" (1 Peter 4:13-14). In 2 Peter 1:4, he said we were "*partakers* of the divine nature."

When Christ truly dwells within us, it will become natural for us to live for God. Let me explain. The Bible says we are partakers of the divine nature. *Natural* is derived from the word *nature.* In other words, we are partakers of the divine natural.

It's natural for a plum tree to bear plums. A plum doesn't say, "Okay, that's it. I'm tired of bearing plums. This year I'm going to bear apples." No matter how hard that plum tree struggles, it can only bear plums. It is by nature—its root, its trunk, its limb, its leaf—a plum tree.

Prior to our conversion, it was natural for us to develop sinful habit patterns. But once Christ came into our lives, those sinful habit patterns were broken. Christ's love indwells, fills, and overflows us. From the depth of our hearts to the surface of our lives, we are Christian.

It is now natural for us to respond as Christ would: To do good to those who despitefully use us, to love our enemies, to turn the other cheek, and to walk the extra mile are all natural.

We have become *partakers* of the "divine nature."

Follow The Leader

Faithful followers recognize Christ's *lordship*. During the time of Napoleon's reign, a young French soldier was shot in the chest during a fierce battle. As the surgeon probed the boy's ribs searching for the bullet, the boy said in his dying breath, "A little deeper, and you will find the Emperor." What he was saying was that at the depth of his heart, he was wholly committed to Napoleon.

Christ wants that same commitment from His followers. When the enemy attacks, we, too, can respond, "A little deeper, and you will find my Lord."

Once a young man walked up to me and said, "I have a problem with drugs."

"No," I said, "you have a problem with *lordship*."

A husband once said, "I have a problem loving my wife as I should."

"No," again I responded, "you have a problem with *lordship.*"

A woman told me, "I can't stand my pastor, and I can't follow his leadership."

I told her, "It's not your pastor. You have a problem with *lordship.*"

When we give our lives to Christ, we give up the rights that we think are ours. Christ gave up His rights and submitted to God's will.

"Let this mind be in you, which was also in Christ Jesus: Who, being in the form of God, thought it not robbery to be equal with God: But made himself of no reputation, and took upon him the form of a servant, and ... humbled himself, and became obedient unto death, even the death of the cross" (Philippians 2:5-8).

That's what discipleship is all about. It's about *rights* and yielding those rights. It's about divine placement and being willing to stay in our place. It's about obedience and learning to love the authority God has given to help us become the person He wants us to be.

Every Christian An Evangelist

Finally, I believe God is looking for each of His children to be an *evangelist* to tell others the good news of Jesus Christ.

After graduation from high school, a Christian man became burdened for his hometown school in Texas. Too bad I've already graduated, he thought. But he couldn't shake the burden. The stirrings remained in his soul.

But this young man had a problem. He was 5'7" and weighed 230 pounds. He wanted to do something for God but felt he was just one big mound of fat. So he went on a diet. Each day he did a few situps and some pushups until he worked himself up to 250 situps a day and 100 pushups. His weight dropped to 140 pounds.

When he was twenty years old, this young man went back to his high school. The principal said, "Who are you?" He could not believe the difference he saw in this person.

The young man said, "You know, sir, there are kids in this school who are like I used to be. They feel intimidated. They feel as though nobody cares or loves them. I'd be willing to come here at lunchtime every day and talk to these students and tell them what happened to me." The principal agreed.

So, every day at noon, this young man went to the school. The first day, he spoke to only a few kids. The next day four or five more came, until around five hundred students were coming to hear him. This young man would tell about his life, how it had changed, and that Jesus was the One who helped him change.

Revival broke out on that high school campus. The principals in the city got together and decided to have this young man speak on a different high school campus each day. Hundreds of students in schools all over the city came to a saving faith in Jesus Christ.

That year, Don Brazille received the Annual City Merit Award from the city council usually awarded to an heroic citizen for service above and beyond the call of duty. They explained, "Don, you have earned this award because you have helped curtail the drug usage problem in our city."

It's easy to drift into a carnal lifestyle when our "spiritual necks" are never on the line. When a Christian fails to witness for Christ, he seldom has to trust God for spiritual strength. Evangelizing at work or school is always a test for the believer.

Are you willing to take the test?

I know God will help you to pass it, but you must be willing to step out first and take it.

D.I.S.C.I.P.L.E.

The eight words that I've used to describe a faithful follower are decision, influence, sacrifice, commitment, integrity, partakers, lordship, and evangelist. Take the first letter of each of these words, and you will find the word *disciple*.

That's what a faithful follower is. A disciple of the Most High God.

Jesus said, "For which of you, intending to build a tower, sitteth not down first, and counteth the cost, whether he have sufficient to finish it?" (Luke 14:28).

God wants us to count the cost of following Him. Are you willing?

Chapter 11

REVOLUTIONARY REVIVAL

I know what it's like to be a church burn-out because I was one. In spite of being raised in the home of John and Bonnie Wilkerson (the best parents God ever made), somehow, the real message of Christ never got to my heart. Around our dinner table, I heard stories from some of the greatest men and women of God. For eighteen years, I heard them and heard them and heard them. Some of the greatest preachers alive today have preached in my father's churches and have talked to me personally. I listened and listened and listened—but it went in one ear and out the other.

In An Alien World

After leaving high school, I enrolled at North Central Bible College in Minneapolis, Minnesota. My attitude didn't change; in fact, it may have gotten worse. Cynicism, sarcasm, and downright sacrilege went on among those of us who attended that school's chapel services.

I'll never forget the day one of the students brought a "laughing machine" to the chapel. You know, one of those gadgets that mechanically makes a sound similar to laughter when you pull the cord. The administrative dean of the school was a very kind man, but we were quite rude to him.

One day this dean stood up to pray for the offering, and my friend pulled the cord on the laughing machine. That machine went on and on, getting wackier and wackier—and the student couldn't get it to stop. That poor dean just kept on praying.

But coming from my background, I knew enough of the gospel to know this was wrong. I sat there waiting for God to shoot lightning through the ceiling and kill us all.

Toward the end of my freshman year, I sang in a group called the "Gospel Hymns"—no girls, just hims! That spring, we traveled around the north central states. Wearing tuxedos and flat-top haircuts, we sang songs such as "A Mighty Fortress Is Our God."

We were doing this during the "hippie movement" when hair was long enough to sit on, and hippies were smoking anything they could roll. One day I walked into a cafe in Minneapolis, and a man was sitting in the corner smoking a bread stick. Honest! He picked up a bread stick from the center of the table, lit it up, and smoked it.

The people to whom we ministered were really polite. But they said things such as, "Who are those guys? Where did they come from? They must be aliens!'' It was a miserable trip. Obviously, the ''Gospel Hymns'' didn't make much of an impact.

A Meeting With God

After ten days on the road and driving all night in an old bus, we got home around 7:00 a.m. one Monday morning. We unpacked the bus, and by 9:00 a.m. I headed over to my father's office before I went home to sleep.

As I walked up the stairs to the church, a middle-aged woman whom I had never seen in my life opened the door and said, ''You must be Rich.'' I didn't even get to say *hi* just *yes*.

She jumped right in. ''Okay, come with me. God has been talking to me all week about you.'' She grabbed my arm and hauled me off to the basement prayer room.

I was thinking, Who is this woman? I hadn't even had a chance to say hello to my father yet. Once we got downstairs, she said, ''God has shown me, Rich, that you have a serious problem on your hands.''

I said, ''Lady, who are you?''

She told me her name was Joy Dawson and continued, ''I held a meeting at your father's church last week. Your father hasn't said anything to me about you, but God told me I was to speak to you before I leave for Houston. There is a major thing going on in your life, and you haven't dealt with it before God.

"Now, listen, take your Bible over in the corner, and God is going to speak to your heart. You get on your knees in that corner, and I'll get on my knees over here. I'm going to pray until God talks to you."

I'll tell you ... this lady was strange! But she was so spiritually strange that I couldn't stand up to her. I was afraid to resist for fear she would pull some whammy on me or something. But I felt like this because I was so rebellious. (Since then, I've come to know that Joy Dawson is a woman whom God uses in mighty and miraculous ways.) So I headed for the corner—ticked off, tired, and upset that I had not yet seen my father.

An Appointed Day

Now let me explain something to you. For every person on this planet, the Bible says, there is coming a day when the Holy Spirit is going to draw you to an appointment with Jesus. When it's your time, you can make the choice to say yes or no to God. Well, this was my day. Before the foundations of the world, God ordained that, in that very room, I was going to have a chance to get right with Him.

From the time I walked away from that woman and got on my knees in that prayer corner, the Holy Ghost of God had broken something up in me. Before my knees hit the floor, I was weeping convulsively and couldn't stop. All of a sudden, God showed me my sin, my rebellion, my callousness, my cynicism, and my sarcasm. I realized in that moment that I had broken the heart of God by my sin. At least thirty minutes went by as I prayed and wept, "Oh, God, forgive me and cleanse me."

Then I began to struggle with what God had told this woman I needed to deal with. My problem was I had no direction regarding what I would do with my life after my first year at Bible college. I didn't want to go back to North Central again. I had not been living for God, and I didn't feel anyone else there was either. "Please, God, don't send me there again," I pleaded. Should I go to the University of Minnesota or get a job and begin to work? I had no idea what God's will was for my life.

And then God gave me a vision. I had never had a vision before, nor have I had one since. I used to be very cynical when someone said they had a vision. But believe me, God got my attention with a vision.

I saw a giant waterfall similar to Niagara Falls. Instead of water pouring over the falls, I saw the letters N.C.B.C.—the first letter of each word for North Central Bible College. Thousands of N's and C's and B's poured over that waterfall as I watched. God was impressing upon my heart and mind to stay at North Central Bible College. As quickly as the vision came, it left.

What a morning! I had gotten off the bus with my life full of sin; and, in just a few hours, my life had completely taken a turnaround. I wondered what in the world was going on and what would happen next. After everything else, I was now seeing visions!

Waiting For Confirmation

When I got up from my knees and walked over to that woman, I said, "Ma'am, I think God talked to me."

"You think?" she said. "Son, you can KNOW. What you need is *scriptural confirmation.*"

I said, "What's that?"

"Scriptural confirmation," she said, "happens when God gives you a scripture from the Bible to back up what He has told you in the Spirit."

"Yes, I guess I do need *scriptural confirmation,*" I said.

"Okay, take my Bible back over to that corner and ask God to confirm His Word to you, and don't come back until He does," she ordered.

As I walked back to my prayer corner, I thought, Please, God, give me *scriptural confirmation* because if You don't, that woman will probably call fire from heaven. Immediately, God dropped this thought into my mind, "Turn to James 4." I had to turn to the table of contents to find what page James was on. At first it didn't make sense until I read the last verse. "Therefore to him that knoweth to do good, and doeth it not, to him it is sin" (James 4:17). It was as though God took a two-by-four and said, "If you don't go back to N.C.B.C., you might as well go out into a life of sin because you'll be sinning by disobeying My word to you today."

So I got up, walked back over to the lady and said, "Excuse me. God just gave me scriptural confirmation."

"Hold it, don't tell me what He said. We're going upstairs to tell your father what your problem was." How could she tell my father, I wondered? I hadn't told her! She went on, "I'm going to tell him what God's answer was and the two reasons why God gave you that answer."

God's Revealed Plan

I followed her up the stairs. But I thought to myself ... for sure, this lady lives right around the corner from the cracker factory. I walked so lightly up those stairs that I never put my full weight down—similar to what I do when I'm on an airplane.

"Pastor Wilkerson," she said as soon as we stepped into my dad's office. "Your son, Rich, has had a big problem in his life."

"What is it, Son?" my dad greeted me.

"Quiet," she interrupted. "I'm going to tell you. Rich has struggled with what to do with his life next year—should he go to the university or stay at N.C.B.C. or get a job?"

I looked at her wide-eyed! "Who told you that?"

"Quiet," she again commanded. "God told me. Furthermore, God just spoke to him in the prayer room—after Rich got his heart right. God told him to stay at N.C.B.C."

Again, I said, "Who told you that?"

"Listen, God told me. Now don't ask anymore. These are the two reasons why God wants Rich to stay at N.C.B.C."

By this time, I was really paying attention. This woman was batting a thousand.

"In the fall of this year," she began, "God is going to send a revival to North Central Bible College that will be unparalleled in its history."

I thought, right away, no way will there be a revival at N.C.B.C. No way! With the laughing machine, and the dean whom everyone made fun of, and the cynicism—no way! This lady must be a false prophetess. I wished she would have stopped while she was still ahead.

"The second reason why God wants Rich at that school is because, in the spring of next year, God is going to send him into full-time ministry."

Okay, now I knew she must be a false prophetess. I had to look in the table of contents to find the book of James. No way could God use me in full-time ministry within a year.

"That's it," she said. "That's the prophecy. I've got to catch my plane. Goodbye."

Whew! She was gone. Good riddance. What a strange person, I thought!

But God did something that day. Even though I discounted her prophecies, I knew God did *something*. I was never the same Rich Wilkerson after that day—never, never, never!

And God Said ...

We had a great summer. I put that experience in the back of my mind. In September school started, and everything was just like it always was. The chapel services were wacky, the guys were

146

cynical, and the attitudes were negative. But it didn't matter because I had become a disciple of Jesus Christ, and no one was going to change that.

But in October something happened. Dick Eastman came to our school for "Spiritual Emphasis Week." This week everyone was supposed to get real spiritual. We scrunched up our faces, making it look as though we were getting used to the light because we had been in the closet praying for fourteen days. People walked around talking real deep and saying Halle-LUJAH a lot. But during Spiritual Emphasis Week the previous year, only twenty-five out of four hundred students preparing for the ministry showed up at the evening meetings.

On the first day, Dick said, "God has shown me on the plane from Sacramento that He's going to do ten things at this school this week." And he started listing them. They were so radical that by the time he got to point three, everybody started to listen. Especially my buddies in the back row. They were saying, "Oh, man, if this stuff really happens, we'll all be dead. And if it doesn't, this man will have been the biggest liar we have heard in our pulpit."

And Revival Came ...

At point seven, Dick stopped. "You, young man," he pointed. "Stand up. You've been involved in ... " and on he went boom, boom, boom describing the terrible sin this guy was tangled in.

147

He had never met this guy before. "Get out in the aisle right now," Dick commanded.

What happened next had already been happening around the country under Katherine Kuhlman's ministry. People were being slain in the Spirit. But we in Minneapolis always got everything about five years late and had never heard of such a thing.

As this young man stepped out into the aisle, Dick ran down to meet him. Dick reached out his hand, touched him, and said, "In the name of Jesus" and pow—this guy went down! He was down, out, flat on his back. The guys in the back were sure God had killed Bobby!

Then Dick turned to another guy and said, "You, over there, stand up."

This kid was watching closely and said, "Oh, no, not me."

Dick said, "You've been involved in this, too." By the time the kid got to the aisle, boom, there he was flat out, in the Spirit, lying on his back.

The guys in the back were now lamenting, "Oh, God. Oh, God."

Before the meeting ended at 6:00 that evening, four hundred and fifty students were flat on their backs, weeping in the presence of God. Not some—all of them!

Word got around fast. The place was jammed to the rafters that night with students and parents from the Minneapolis area who had heard what had happened. There were not enough aluminum chairs to set up, and people lined the walls of that administration building.

On Wednesday, all five floors of that old building were jammed with people. Loudspeakers were placed so people could hear in the hallways. The meetings all ended the same way—people praying for other people and boom—flat out in the Spirit. All classes had been canceled. A Holy Ghost revival was shaking that place.

And God Reminded Me ...

On Wednesday night, around 3:00 a.m., I went to the chapel. About six hundred people were there praying and singing in the Spirit. And they were all through the hallways and through all five floors of the building.

I sat there quietly for a while taking it all in. Then God spoke to me. "Rich, do you remember when My servant came to you this past spring and prophesied this was going to happen? You didn't believe her, did you, son?" I fell out of my chair and onto the floor. I said to God, "God, may I never doubt Your word again."

A lot of positive things happened after that week. Students were out preaching the gospel and singing around our five-state area. The spirit of revival is still going on at N.C.B.C. with worldwide ramifications. The school has tripled in size since those days.

Prophecy: Part Two

In February of that year, I traveled with a singing group. When I got back to my parent's home after one of the tours, there was a note stuck to my phone. "Uncle Ira called yesterday and wants you to call him as soon as you get in."

Early the next morning, I called my uncle who pastored a church in Ft. Worth, Texas.

"Rich," he greeted me, "God's been moving here among our young people, and our youth director is getting ready to leave as a missionary to East Africa. We've heard about the revival at your school and what God has done. Would you consider coming down and becoming our full-time youth minister? You could finish your education at Southwestern College."

I said, "Ah, Uncle Ira, give me a break. There is no way I could do that. I'm too young. I'm only nineteen, and it's been only in the past six months that I've gotten interested in God's Word. Sometimes I still have to look in the table of contents. Some of your young people are probably older than I am. Sorry, there is no way."

"Listen," he went on, "why don't you just get on the plane at Easter and come down and check it out. We'll pay for your ticket."

So I went and met the young people and the church board. On the way back to the airport, Uncle Ira said, "Well, how about it? Will you pray and call me in about two weeks?"

I prayed for eleven days—sought God on my knees every night and every morning. For all eleven days, it seemed the windows of heaven were shut. On the eleventh night, I asked my roommate, Terry Kirschman, to pray with me. I really pressed him to pray. I kept saying, "But I'd do it for you."

I'm glad God gave me an answer or Terry may still be there on his knees praying—that's what kind of commitment he made to me. So we cried out to God for spiritual direction.

After about thirty minutes of lying flat out on my face before God, I once again sensed the voice of the Holy Spirit. God reminded me of the second part of the prophecy I had received almost a year earlier in my father's church in the corner of the basement.

By now I knew enough to ask for *scriptural confirmation*. The Lord led me to the first chapter of Jeremiah that describes the call of God upon the life of the young prophet. Many theologians believe he may have been between the ages of sixteen and twenty-two at the time.

The Word of God came to Jeremiah saying, "Before I formed thee in the belly I knew thee; and before thou cameth forth out of the womb I sanctified thee, and I ordained thee a prophet unto the nations." And Jeremiah answered, "Ah, Lord God! behold, I cannot speak: for I am a child" (Jeremiah 1:5-6).

That's what I was telling God. Isn't it wild that God chose to show me another young man in history that had been going through the same struggle!

I answered the call of God that night—called my uncle and said, "I'm coming!"

Don't tell me God doesn't speak to us directly. I want you to know God hears and *answers* prayer. Even though that incident happened years ago in my life, it's as fresh in my memory as if it happened yesterday.

God can send revival again and again and again to change those whom He intends to use.

Holy Ghost Revolution

Revolutionary revival will burn the dross of sin out of a person's heart. It's a sure-fire solution to turning back the spirit of carnality. Revival always produces holiness and a longing to please God first and foremost.

The corporate church is galvanized into a forward moving army of God when revival comes. You can study under the finest Bible theologians and preachers, but I'd rather have a revolutionary revival. You can watch thousands of non-stop, no commercial, Christian television shows, but I'd still rather have a Holy Ghost revolutionary revival. You can train at the finest Bible colleges and seminaries for Christian training today, but I'd rather have a revolutionary revival from God.

I believe in powerful preaching and teaching, Christian television, Bible colleges and seminaries, and other needed Christian ministries, but I have learned that it's all sounding brass and tinkling symbols without the agape love that flows in the midst of a revolutionary revival.

Revolutionary revival also produces men and women who are willing to go into all the world for Christ. There will always be recruits following revival. When revival hit N.C.B.C., students just couldn't do enough or give enough or go enough for God. They wanted to serve Him.

Love, Joy, Peace, And More

All through my growing years, I heard preachers say, "Accept Jesus and you will have peace, love, joy, and more." More? I always wondered what the *more* was. Was it Cadillacs, diamonds, and money? Was it fancy cars and gold jewelry?

I believe I've learned what the *more* is. It's the *cross!*

Yes, Jesus came to give us peace—peace that passes all understanding. Peace that the world cannot possibly understand. He gave us a love so deep that it has taken some into the deepest jungles of India and Africa and into the streets of Chicago and New York City. He's given us love for people who don't love us.

God has given joy to some whose backs have been bloodied by the whips of their torturers—joy that flows so deep into the cisterns of the soul that the world cannot explain.

But God has called us to far more than that. He has called us to take up our cross and follow Him. Jesus said we cannot be His disciple if we will not take up our cross and follow.

You've been taught incorrectly if you think life as a Christian is going to be wonderful, wonderful, wonderful. It will be *spiritually* wonderful, because our enemy, Satan, no longer has control over us. We have become children of the King and have been made victorious.

But if the message of the cross has been omitted, you are in error.

Do you have a hard time believing that? Then let's look back at Christ's original twelve disciples. Ten out of the original twelve disciples died a martyr's death. Talk to them about the big bucks, the diamonds, and the gold.

Suspended between heaven and earth, Christ hung on the cross. Historians tell us His pectoral muscles went into spasms causing His lungs to freeze so He could not inhale or exhale. The only way Christ could exhale was to pull up on the nails in His hands or push on the nails in His feet, ripping flesh as He pushed. When He could stand the pain no longer, He dropped again until His muscles froze and went into another spasm.

Stephen, a young man of God, stood one day in history and preached an anointed message to the Jews. When he had finished, the crowd had two choices. They could fall on their knees in repentance or stone the speaker. They chose the latter. Stephen was pelted with stones until he fell into the hands of Jesus.

Thomas had a spear driven through him in India. Luke was hung on a tree in Greece. Mark was dragged to his death in Alexandria. James the Great was beheaded in Judea. Paul was beheaded in Rome. James the Less, the brother of Jesus, had his brains beat out at the age of ninety-four because he served Jesus. John was boiled in oil.

Peter was crucified upside down. His wife was nailed to a cross as Peter watched them torture her. Historians tell us his last words to his wife were, "A little while longer, and we'll sing songs around the throne of the Almighty God." Peter's last request was that they hang him upside down on the cross because he felt he was not worthy to be crucified as was his Lord—and history tells us that is exactly how he died.

And Still More

Those Bible characters followed Christ thousands of years ago. What about those who have served since then? Did you ever hear of Sovanarola? He was a Catholic monk from the fifteenth century. Catholicism was known more during his time for its torture chambers than its prayer rooms.

Sovanarola preached the gospel in St. Mark's Church in Florence, Italy, to thousands of people. He refused to compromise the truth of God's Word.

One day the authorities from Rome dragged this man out of the pulpit, down the center aisle, and out the back door. They put him on a stretching rack in prison. Day after day, he would be taken from this stretching rack outside. With a rope, they would pull him up and then drop him from a twelve-foot pole ten to fifteen times a day. After weeks of this torture, Sovanarola's body was crushed and broken. Do you think they would let him die in peace? No! They took that little man of God to the center of the city, wrapped his ankles to a stake, and built a kindling at his feet. As the town watched, he burned to death.

One of the church leaders called down from a balcony, "From the church militant and the church triumphant we excommunicate you. We throw you out and cut you off."

Historians say this man raised his bruised and broken head one final time. He summoned every last ounce of strength for one final message. It was one of the greatest one-sentence messages history has recorded.

This one-liner has taken young people out of their comfortable churches and placed them on the mission fields in the darkest places of this world. It has encouraged pastors, taken them out of depression, and set them back on the Rock— Jesus Christ.

Sovanarola said, in one last dying breath, "Sir, from the church militant maybe, but from the church of Jesus Christ triumphant—never, never, never."

We can never be thrown out of the Church triumphant. Hallelujah! Why? Because two thousand years ago, Jesus Christ looked at Peter and said, "Upon this rock I will build my church and the gates of hell shall not prevail against it." Hallelujah! Hallelujah!

Exchanging Rags For Riches

After eight years in youth work, God led me into evangelism. During those eight years, my wife Robyn and I had it all. I know I was one of the highest paid youth workers on the West Coast in 1978. Robyn was the vice-president of a mortgage banking firm. Together we made over $55,000 a year. We had a beautiful home, pool, jacuzzi, and an orange Corvette—all for the glory of God. Now there is nothing wrong with having *things*. But when those things have you, you are no longer of use to the kingdom. That's what was happening to me.

One afternoon, I was alone in my office, and the Spirit of God began to deal with me. I heard in my spirit these words, "Rich, is this what you want? Because, son, if the cars and houses and land and money is what you want, I'll give it to you. I own it all, and you can have it. But, Rich, if you let Me, I'd like to show you a part of life you know nothing about. It can be far more exciting."

"What is it, God?" I asked with excitement.

"I'd like you to march into My cross and know what it means to pay the price," He answered.

I was tired, so tired. Ministering outside the will of God, in the flesh, can make a person weary. Tears streamed down my face that afternoon as I said to God, "Yes, God, that's what I want. Take this *stuff*. I'd rather have You." A fresh, revolutionary revival began to happen in my life that day in 1979.

Within two weeks, Robyn and I were gone. Two weeks! Within a month, our house was sold, and all our belongings were sold, given away, or stored. We were on the road preaching the Gospel within a four-week period. All we had to our name was a car payment. We had no income, no booking agents, no promotions, no one to set up book tables—nothing. Nothing except a *mandate* from God.

I remember a night, early in our ministry, when we pulled into town and stayed in a dirty little motel. I got up early the next morning to meet with a pastor and the local principals to set up appointments for high school assemblies. Robyn slipped out of bed, got down on her knees, and said, "Rich, while you go to speak to those principals, I'll be right here on my knees praying that God will open doors that no man can close."

God continues to answer my wife's prayers. At this writing, I've spoken to nearly a million students in over one thousand public school assemblies. That's over fifty thousand converts ago. I've been laughed at by principals, rejected by teachers, and cursed by students, but I'm still excited about my experience with the cross of Christ.

In the last seven years, our ministry has exploded. Twelve people work with us in our ministry now. We have 15,000 people on our mailing list, and our work load has become excessive. But if God wanted to take all of this away tomorrow, I would say, "Take it, God. It's all Yours anyhow. But, God, don't take away the experience of the cross or Your blessed Holy Spirit."

A Message From A Servant On His Way Home

In the summer of 1981, my friend Keith Green and I sat in his home and prayed. You could not spend much time with Keith without soon being in prayer. He said, "Rich, whatever you hear about me in the coming days, remember one thing. I've pledged my head for the Gospel. I will give everything for this marvelous message to get out—no matter what it costs me." We spent the rest of the day together, praying, crying, and praying some more.

In the summer of 1982, Keith and I were speakers at the *Jesus West Coast* conference. I was the opening night speaker, and Keith was the closing night speaker. That last concert is now history. Many of you, I'm sure, have seen the videotape of that concert.

Three weeks later, I woke up at 2:00 a.m.—wide awake as though it were noon—singing one of Keith's songs. The words went like this:

> My eyes are dry, my faith is old,
> My heart is hard, my prayers are cold,
> And I know how I ought to be ...
> Alive to You and dead to me.
> Oh, what can be done
> For an old heart like mine?
> Soften it up with oil and wine.
> The oil is You, Your Spirit of love.
> Please wash me anew
> In the wine of Your blood.[1]

I fell asleep. At 6:30 a.m. the phone rang. "Oh, Rich," my secretary said weeping, "did you hear the news about Keith Green? He and two of his children, along with another family, were killed in a plane crash."

"It must be a mistake," I said. "It can't be true."

"No, Rich, it's true. It's all over the radio stations. They're gone."

I awakened my wife, and we knelt by the bed, crying, praying, and remembering Keith's words of absolute commitment to Jesus.

Take Up Your Cross

Our medical and law schools are bursting at their seams.

God knows we don't need more lawyers. This planet can't keep the ten commandments much less what those people have added on.

Our educational field is overrun, and some teachers can't find jobs.

What is needed are Holy Ghost anointed men and women who are willing to take up the cross of Jesus Christ and pay the price of discipleship. Men and women who are willing to bleed and die if necessary for the cause of Christ. We don't have enough recruits for the work of the Lord.

Maybe some of you reading this book have been struggling with something you know is not the will of God for your life. Maybe someone has strongly influenced your decision, and you're following that suggestion—and running from the call of God.

Maybe some of you are just plain sick of all the compromising you've been doing in your Christian walk. You've had it!

Then why not say to God, "Just once, God, I want to be that man/woman of God that You have in mind for me. Just once, God."

Taking up your cross will cost you—your time, your allegiance, your attention, your money, and everything you have, own, hope to be, were, and shall be.

Here's what to do. Get down on your knees right now with your Bible. Open your heart to God and repeat the words I quoted from Keith Green's song.

God will do the rest. You will experience a "Revolutionary Revival!"

Chapter 12

MOUNTAIN-MOVING MINISTRIES

Throughout the second half of this book, I've been giving you suggestions for moving out of carnality and into a closer relationship with God. I've talked about experiencing complete confession and radical repentance, becoming a prayer warrior, following faithfully after God, and carrying one's own cross in order to produce revolutionary revival.

I'd like to conclude by offering hope to those who may be saying, "Oh, no, not me. God can never use me." I hear those same words time and time again from dejected, defeated, and despairing people.

Reason Number One

Past sin—lingering in one's mind—is the number one reason people believe they are unacceptable in God's service. I'm talking about the sins already confessed, already forgiven by God, but still remembered by that person. Listen, when it comes to *forgiven* sin, God has a terrible memory.

God said, "I, yes, I alone am he who blots away your sins for my own sake and will never think of them again" (Isaiah 43:25 *TLB*). "Oh, return to me, for I have paid the price to set you free" (Isaiah 44:22 *TLB*).

Rahab, the prostitute, is one of the best examples of forgiveness in the Bible. When Joshua sent two of his men into Jericho to spy out the land, Rahab was the one who gave them safety in her home and helped them escape. Later, when Israel came in and overthrew Jericho, her family was the only one spared. God saw promise in Rahab's life.

Matthew 1:5 records Rahab's name as part of Christ's geneology. Think of it! A prostitute as part of Christ's heritage—forgiven, made whole, and used by God.

Rahab the prostitute, Peter the liar, and Saul the accomplice to murder are all proof that God forgives and forgets *past* sin.

Reason Number Two

This reason is often given by someone with a *martyr complex.* "I'm no good, I'm ugly, I'm broke, or I have nothing to offer God." What a lie Satan has spread to make Christians believe they've got to be "somebody" before they can help "anybody." God is not asking you to give Him what you don't have. He's asking you to work with what He has already given you.

Television creates a fantasy world of beauty—homes, cars, families, and individual lives. Unfortunately, even Christian broadcasting has been affected. Daily, Christian networks feature God's beautiful people either doing aerobic dancing or discussing topics such as "face lifts, male impotence, or household organization."

The Christian television stars wear the newest fashions. They feature on their programs great singers, great preachers, and great interviewers. It's all great! But what about the little Christian watching who thinks he is too fat or too short or too skinny or too something else?

A great and mighty man of God once thought of himself as a "word fumbler." Moses said to God, "O my Lord, I am not eloquent, neither heretofore, nor since thou hast spoken unto thy servant: but I am slow of speech, and of a slow tongue" (Exodus 4:10).

Some theologians believe that perhaps Moses had a speech impediment. But whether it was obvious to others or only to himself, Moses felt inadequate for the job.

An old saying is still true. "He whom God calls, God also equips."

God was not looking for a great speaker. He was looking for a man with a great heart.

God said, "Moses, I'll send your brother Aaron to be your spokesman." And Moses yielded to God's will. While in the "world's eye" Moses had little to offer, He was willing to give God what he did have.

That old "word fumbler" became God's great deliverer, and the rest is history.

Reason Number Three

Another reason for delaying service to God may be the excuse, "Not only am *I* inadequate, but so are my *financial resources.*"

In Acts 3, Peter and John, two "penniless" men went to the temple to pray. As they passed the Gate Beautiful, a man lame from birth asked them for money. "Then Peter said, Silver and gold have I none; but such as I have give I thee: In the name of Jesus Christ of Nazareth rise up and walk" (Acts 3:6).

The Bible records that this man went walking and leaping and praising God throughout the temple. Nowhere can we read that this man said to Peter or John,"You know, I would rather have had a couple of bucks than this healing." No way! That man needed a touch from God!

This world isn't looking for money, it needs a miracle. People don't need diamonds. They need deliverance. A handout is not as appreciated as a helping hand.

Christians have the message that can set captives free, and it's not found in money.

Material gain must never keep us from serving the God who owns "the cattle upon a thousand hills" (Psalm 50:10). It is God's problem to supply our needs; our problem is learning to obey when He calls.

If Christians are to destroy the work of the enemy, then we must decide it is time to stop making excuses and get on with it. God *can* and *will* use all of us in His service as He sees best. Each of us must find out for ourselves what that service must be.

Work With All Thy Might

First, consider the following verses from the *Living Bible.*

"Now here is a command, dear brothers, given in the name of our Lord Jesus Christ by his authority: Stay away from any Christian who spends his days in laziness and does not follow the ideal of hard work we set up for you. For you well know that you ought to follow our example: you never saw us loafing" (2 Thessalonians 3:6-7 *TLB*).

"So, my dear brothers, since future victory is sure, be strong and steady, always abounding in the Lord's work, for you know that nothing you do for the Lord is ever wasted as it would be if there were no resurrection" (1 Corinthians 15:58 *TLB*).

"I strain to reach the end of the race and receive the prize for which God is calling us" (Philippians 3:14 *TLB*).

My friend, it is high time that we roll up our sleeves and begin to work for God. Our task is not to find the appropriate paint for the hallowed hallways of our spacious cathedrals, but rather to go into the highways and byways and compel the lost to come to Jesus.

Listen to Solomon's words: "Whatsoever thy hand findeth to do, do it with thy might" (Ecclesiastes 9:10).

Work As Unto The Lord

I've grown weary hearing adults complain, "She gets to do more solos than I do." Or, "Why didn't I get asked to be on that committee?" Or, "His name is on his door. Why isn't mine on my door?" Or, "The church called a prayer meeting, and only two of us showed up. Boy, did we feel stupid kneeling there by ourselves." Oh, God, help us!

Hearing these statements makes others think we serve God only for worldly applause. God forbid!

Jesus said, "Then these righteous ones will reply, 'Sir, when did we ever see you hungry and feed you? Or thirsty and give you anything to drink? Or a stranger, and help you? Or naked, and clothe you? When did we ever see you sick or in prison, and visit you?' And I the King will tell them, 'When you did it to these my brothers you were doing it to me'" (Matthew 25:37-40 *TLB*).

Paul said, "And whatever you do or say, let it be as a representative of the Lord Jesus, and come with him into the presence of God the Father to give him your thanks.... Work hard and cheerfully at all you do, just as though you were working for the Lord and not merely for your masters, remembering that it is the Lord Christ who is going to pay you, giving you your full portion of all he owns. He is the one you are really working for" (Colossians 3:17,23-24 *TLB*).

There you have it. God demands that our labor be unto the Lord. If someone else gets the credit here on earth, we are to stand back and applaud them. Remember ... DO YOUR WORK AS UNTO THE LORD.

Recognize The Difficulty

A life lived for God is beyond all doubt the most fulfilling life ever imagined. Yet, no life could be more demanding.

Ten of the original twelve apostles died a martyr's death. Through the centuries, men and women have toiled hard in difficult surroundings to give the Gospel to lost souls.

Victor Pymire, one of the first western missionaries to Tibet, worked for fourteen years before he had his first convert.

Cary worked for seven years before he baptized his first convert in India.

Judson did not win his first disciple in Burma before seven years.

Morrison, in China, and Henry Richards, in Banza, Mateka, also worked for seven years before they won a soul to Christ.

What price are you willing to pay to see the Gospel made known? Whether you are on the job, at school, out on the street, in military service, or in a remote jungle, what price will you pay?

> Ne'er think the victory won
> Nor lay thine armor down.
> The fight of faith will not be done
> Till thou obtain the crown.

For Such A Time As This

Long ago, in a Persian empire, Esther, a Jewish woman, became the queen through divine intervention. Her people (the Jews) faced extinction because of a strange edict signed by the king himself. Their only hope was for Esther to go before the king and plead for mercy—even though it may have cost Esther her life.

Her Uncle Mordecai wrote to her saying, "Do you think you will escape there in the palace, when all other Jews are killed? If you keep quiet at a time like this, God will deliver the Jews from some other source, but you and your relatives will die; what's more, who can say but that God has brought you into the palace for just such a time as this?" (Esther 4:13-14 *TLB*).

Esther responded, and her people were saved. She had been brought into the kingdom for such a time as this!

In our own family, we have a dynamic man of God, Dr. Mark Buntain, my wife's uncle. In 1955, God called Dr. Buntain, his wife, and their tiny child to Calcutta, India. At this writing, approximately eleven million people live in Calcutta, and about three million of them live on the streets. I mean *on* the streets! They conceive, give birth, eat, sleep, bathe, beg, and die on the streets.

During his first four years in Calcutta, Dr. Buntain preached seven nights a week in a little storefront building. Many times only his wife and baby girl attended. People would sometimes walk by and curse them, spit on them, or throw things at them. But Mark, Huldah, and Bonnie persevered.

Before long they began a feeding program, a medical program, and several churches. Today, over thirty years later, Mark Buntain oversees seven different language congregations with over ten thousand people attending.

His ministry feeds over twenty-five thousand children the only meal they get each day. Nearly eight thousand children are enrolled in the K-12 Christian school.

Over nine hundred people are currently employed through their ministry in Calcutta. Dr. Buntain's six-story hospital with one hundred and twenty beds is known for the high quality of patient care. Even Mother Teresa takes patients to Dr. Buntain's hospital.

In addition to medical work, the ministry teaches over four hundred thousand correspondents in their Bible training courses throughout the nation of India.

In 1976, my wife and I were privileged to take ten young men to Calcutta to see this great work. From the time our plane landed until we finally got to where we were staying, all twelve of us wept. We could not believe the depth of one man's commitment to Jesus Christ.

What if Mark and Huldah Buntain had not gone to Calcutta?

What if you don't go where God sends you? What if ... ?

Here Am I—Send Me

Recently, on my way home to Seattle, I changed planes in Salt Lake City, Utah. About fifty young Mormon students got on that plane to go to

Seattle, enroute to Japan. Each had on a nice sport coat, slacks or skirt, white shirt, and a name tag on their lapel with their name in English and in Japanese. These Mormons had just completed two years of training in the culture and language of Japan and were now on their way to a nation where less than one percent professes Christianity.

What if we say, "I don't have time. Let the Mormons go"?

While all this diabolical dogma is being spread all over the world, fundamental Christian churches struggle to keep their young people coming to church.

Father God once asked, "Whom shall I send and who will go for us?" The response from Isaiah was, "Then said I, Here am I; send me" (Isaiah 6:8).

"For such a time as this," God is calling Christians to step out of their carnal, worldly, self-centered lifestyles into an exciting and fulfilling walk with Him.

Oh, how God longs to hear men and women answer as Isaiah did. "Lord, I'll go! Send me!"

How will you now respond to His call?

NOTES

Chapter 1

1. Richard Foster, *Money, Sex and Power* (San Francisco, CA: Harper & Row, 1985), p. 5.

2. Warren W. Wiersbe, *The Best of A.W. Tozer* (Harrisburg, PA: Christian Publications, Inc., 1978), p. 97.

3. A.W. Tozer, *The Pursuit of God* (Harrisburg, PA: Christian Publications, Inc., 1958), p. 20.

Chapter 4

1. Helen Hosier, *The Other Side of Divorce* (Nashville, TN: Abingdon Press, 1975), p. 186-187.

2. John MacArthur, *The Family* (Chicago, IL: Moody, 1982), p. 107.

Chapter 5

1. Winkie Pratney, *Youth Aflame* (Sebastopol, CA: Communication Foundation Publishers, 1970), p. 172.

2. Watchman Nee, *The Normal Christian Life* (Wheaton, IL: Tyndale House, 1977)

3. Elisabeth Elliot, *The Journals of Jim Elliot* (Old Tappan, NJ: Fleming H. Revell, 1978), p. 208.

4. Walter Searle, *David Brainerd's Personal Testimony* (Grand Rapids, MI: Baker Book House, 1978), p. 18.

Chapter 9

1. R. A. Torrey, *How To Pray* (Springdale, PA: Whitaker House, 1983) p. 12-13.

2. E. M. Bounds, *Power Through Prayer* (Springdale, PA: Whitaker House, 1982) p. 31.

Chapter 11

1. "My Eyes Are Dry" by Keith Green from *No Compromise,* ©1978 by Birdwing Music/Ears To Hear Music/Cherry Lane Music Publishing Co. Inc. Used by permission.

FOR FURTHER INFORMATION

Contact:

Rich Wilkerson Crusades
P. O. Box 1092
Tacoma, Washington 98401